THE
DUMOND
AFFAIR

HOW LIES AND POLITICS
FREED A KILLER

D.R. BARTLETTE

WILD BLUE
PRESS

WildBluePress.com

THE DUMOND AFFAIR published by:
WILDBLUE PRESS
P.O. Box 102440
Denver, Colorado 80250

WILDBLUE PRESS is registered at the U.S. Patent and Trademark Offices.

ISBN 978-1-964730-35-6 Hardcover
ISBN 978-1-964730-33-2 Trade Paperback
ISBN 978-1-964730-34-9 eBook

Interior Formatting and Book Cover Design by Elijah Toten
www.totencreative.com

THE
DUMOND
AFFAIR

Contents

Intro – Washington, D.C.

Comet Ping Pong doesn't particularly stand out. For the most part, it blends in with the other cafes and art galleries on Connecticut Avenue in Washington, D.C. The outdoor seating area, which takes up about half of the wide pedestrian sidewalk in front of the shop, is nearly obscured by a wall of potted plants. But it does have one eye-catching feature: a large retro neon sign, originally made for Comet Liquor, that co-founder James Alefantis discovered at a flea market and "couldn't live without."

Inside, its true hipster appeal becomes clearer. Designed by the architectural firm Core, the award-winning interior features layers of colorful plaster on the walls, polished concrete floors, and sixteen-foot ceilings with exposed timber beams and skylights. The booths are made with reclaimed wood seats, and a "sculptural" pizza oven anchors the bar.[1]

But it's not just about the aesthetic – Comet Ping Pong has been ranked among the best pizza joints in D.C. by local food critics. It's also been featured in national publications like *Food & Wine* and *Southern Living*, as well as a 2010 episode of Guy Fieri's *Diners, Drive-Ins, and Dives*, where he said their calzones were "some of the best I've ever had."[2]

Besides serving brunch and a nice selection of craft brews (natch), Comet regularly hosts live music. And, of course, they have ping-pong tables.

While it's a popular local establishment – waits for a table on the weekends can be pretty long[3] – it wasn't really known much outside of D.C. That is, until 2016.

Not long before the November election, Alefantis' Instagram posts and DMs started getting flooded with comments with some of the most hateful and ugly things you can imagine. Hundreds of strangers were suddenly accusing him of being a pedophile and child trafficker. He started receiving death threats. Soon the accusations and threats were showing up on all his social media, as well as those of Comet Ping Pong and its staff.[4]

That's how he discovered #Pizzagate, "an insanely complicated, made-up, fictional lie-based story" alleging that the Clintons and John Podesta, among others, were performing Satanic rituals and running a child sex trafficking out of the basement of Comet Ping Pong (which doesn't actually have a basement).[5]

Alefantis and others in the "reality-based community" thought it had to be a joke – but the accusations and death threats were very real.

Alefantis said he reached out to Facebook and Twitter to get them to take down the unhinged content, to no avail. He said he reached out to the police and FBI, but that went nowhere, too.[6]

Confused as to why he was being targeted by what was clearly a "coordinated political attack," Alefantis did some sleuthing to try and figure out what was going on.

* * *

According to cybersecurity experts interviewed by *Rolling Stone*, the conspiracy theory that would eventually mutate into Pizzagate first emerged in July of 2016. That's when a 4chan user called FBIAnon, who claimed to be a "high-level analyst and strategist" for the FBI, hosted an Ask Me

Anything. In it, they claimed that the Clintons liked foreign donors "so much" because they would "pay in children as well as money" and that Hillary Clinton had sexually abused captive girls.[7]

Then, near the end of October, the conspiracy theory spread to other platforms, including Reddit and TheeRANT, an anonymous message board for New York City police. Someone using the handle Fatoldman posted that he had a "hot rumor" about the FBI investigation into Hillary Clinton's emails. He claimed the FBI had been forced to re-open the case because the NYPD's sex crimes unit had to get involved.[8]

Apparently, someone then shared that post to a law enforcement group on Facebook, where a user called Carmen Katz saw it.

Again according to *Rolling Stone*, the first Facebook post featuring "#Pizzagate" appeared on October 29, 2016, the day after then-FBI Director James Comey announced the bureau would be reopening its investigation into Hillary Clinton's use of a private email server while she was secretary of state.[9] Part of that investigation included data found on Anthony Weiner's laptop, including several references to Comet Ping Pong and Alefantis – a Democrat who donated to both Obama's and Hillary Clinton's presidential campaigns (and ex-boyfriend of David Brock, a former right-wing operative turned Democrat).[10]

On Facebook, Katz posted, "My NYPD source said its [sic] much viler and more serious than classified material on Weiner's device. The email DETAIL [sic] the trips made by Weiner, Bill and Hillary on their pedophile billionaire friend's plane, the Lolita Express. Yup, Hillary has a well-documented predilection for underage girls.... We're talking an international child enslavement and sex ring."[11]

Within twelve hours of Katz's post, Twitter account @ DavidGoldbergNY – which is, in all likelihood, a bot – tweeted a screenshot of her post twice, with the caption, "I've been hearing the same thing from my NYPD buddies." One of those tweets was retweeted almost 6,400 times.[12]

Soon #Pizzagate was being shared and reposted millions of times – including by more than 3,000 accounts that were likely bots. Some of the most frequent #Pizzagate tweeters were linked with Russia's Internet Research Agency.[13]

Nearly six dozen people associated with the 2016 Trump campaign followed several of these Russian accounts pushing #Pizzagate, further spreading it.[14]

But what pushed Pizzagate from social media into a much wider real-world audience was – who else? – Alex Jones. Immediately after the Katz post, and for the next three days, episodes on his show, *Infowars*, were titled "Hillary Clinton Goes Full Tinfoil-Hat," "Hillary Clinton Lifelong Rape Enabler," and "Hillary's Plans to Rig Election Leaked."

On the November 2 episode, aired just four days after the Katz post, he hosted fellow webcaster and conspiracy theorist Douglas Hagmann. In front of an audience of nearly eight million people, Hagmann accused Hillary Clinton of participating in Epstein's sex-trafficking plane, Lolita Express.

As unhinged as this segment was, it wasn't anything out of the ordinary for *Infowars*. Jones has long spread hateful conspiracy theories about the Clintons. He's called Hillary "evil" and "an abject, psychopathic demon" and has accused her of raping and murdering children. "When I think about all the children Hillary Clinton has personally murdered and chopped up and raped, I have zero fear standing up against her," Jones said in a YouTube video posted on November 4, 2016 (which has since been deleted). "Yeah, you heard me right. Hillary Clinton has personally murdered children."[15]

His Pizzagate push even continued after the election: his November 23 episode was titled "Pizzagate is Real." Only four days later, he spent a half hour explaining the conspiracy theory on his show before releasing a separate video titled "Down the #Pizzagate Rabbit Hole." His December 1 episode was titled, "Pizzagate: The Bigger Picture."[16]

***

One of Jones' millions of followers was a soft-spoken – yet "manic"[17] – North Carolina man named Edgar Maddison Welch. The twenty-eight-year-old divorced father of two had lived a life scarred by the death of children and held together with a calling to save them.

When he was only eight, his sixteen-year-old brother lost control of his car and died in the resulting crash. The loss, understandably, devastated his family. His mother, who had been a nurse, changed careers to become a firefighter – an even more immediate way to rescue people. The family began to obsess over saving those more vulnerable – running a no-kill dog shelter, taking in foster children, and sending money to needy children abroad.[18]

For example, in 2010, he went on a mission trip to Haiti. He was apparently devastated by the poverty he saw there. His father would later write a letter to the court stating that before Welch left Haiti, he would call home and plead "to let him bring three or four of the children home and let them live with us."[19]

He later moved to Wilmington to attend community college and study filmmaking. There, along with a few others, he made a short art film titled *Mute*. In it, a troubled young man goes through his day not being heard or understood by anyone around him, until he comes upon a similarly lonely young woman who takes his hand. The film ends with the two walking off into the sunset.[20]

But Welch did not walk off into a happy ending. Instead, he ended up becoming addicted to drugs and dropping out of college. To his credit, he went to rehab and got sober. It's not known exactly what kind of rehab he went to, but afterwards, his friends said he got "aggressively" religious, to the point of screaming in people's faces.[21]

It also didn't seem to help him with his underlying issues. By 2016, his life appeared to be falling apart. He'd dropped out of college. His marriage was over. He'd tried to become a volunteer firefighter, but dropped out of that as well. Broke and aimless, he ended up moving back to his hometown of Salisbury, which he called "Smallsbury."[22]

Then things got even worse. In the fall of that year, he was driving to work when he struck a thirteen-year-old boy, severely injuring him. Welch rendered first aid to the boy, who had to be airlifted to a hospital. While the boy survived, he suffered broken bones and a head injury. Welch wasn't charged, but friends say he was deeply shaken by the incident.[23]

At some point, likely during his stint in rehab, Welch had sworn off the internet, believing he'd become addicted to it. But by the fall of 2016, he had gotten service re-installed and had gone right back to his former compulsive ways. He started consuming *Infowars* "obsessively," along with anything else he could find about Pizzagate.

He texted some of this to his girlfriend in December, stating, "Looking up on pizza gate and it makes me [expletive] sick." She told him to stop consuming Pizzagate content.[24]

But he didn't take her advice. Finally, predictably, he felt like he needed to take action to save the children he believed were being victimized by Hillary Clinton and other elites. He reached out to friends to try and get them to come along with him for what he said would be a "raid" on a "pedo ring," saying it would involve "sacraficing [sic] the lives of a few for the lives of many ... Standing up against a corrupt system that kidnaps, tortures and rapes babies and children in our own backyard."[25]

His friends declined his offer and sort of laughed it off. Welch, after all, had always been the type to "do his own research," and had subscribed to conspiracy theories for years, including 9/11 "truthers." "I don't think he has very much faith in the media, but none of us do," an old friend of his told the *Washington Post*.[26]

On the morning of Sunday, December 6, he told his family he "had some things to do" and set out on the 350-mile drive to D.C. to "have a closer look" and "shine some light on it." He brought an AR-15 and a Colt .38 with him to, in his words, "help rescue children."[27]

During the drive, he recorded a video for his daughters. In it, he says he "can't let you growing up in a world that's so corrupt by evil," and that he has a "duty to protect those who can't protect themselves."[28]

He arrived at Comet just before three that afternoon, when the restaurant was still fairly busy – including with kids who were there playing ping pong.

Welch strode in carrying the AR-15, the .38 strapped to his thigh, and a folding knife in his pocket. He fired the rifle into the air. Then, as the customers and staff fled in terror for their lives, he calmly walked around "investigating," moving furniture around and heading to the back of the restaurant. There, he shot the lock off a door, which only opened to a closet full of kitchen supplies. He then broke through another door, which only led outside to an alley.

It didn't take long for the police to barricade the street and surround the building. Within a short period of time, Welch surrendered peacefully. He freely told police why he had come there. Even after his arrest, when talking to a reporter from the *New York Times*, he conceded that the "intel wasn't one hundred percent" about Comet Ping Pong specifically, but he still believed in the underlying conspiracy theory that Hillary Clinton and other prominent Democrats were running a child sex trafficking ring – if not at Comet Ping Pong, then somewhere else.

As if to back him up, Michael Flynn Jr., the son of Trump adviser (and convicted liar) Gen. Michael Flynn, would share Jack Posobiec's tweet quoting the D.C. police chief as saying there was "nothing to suggest" that Welch "had anything to do with #Pizzagate." Flynn Jr. would comment in his retweet, "Until #Pizzagate proven to be false, it'll remain a story."[29]

Flynn Jr. resigned (or was forced out) immediately afterwards. Welch would end up pleading guilty to federal charges of assault with a dangerous weapon and transporting a firearm over state lines and was sentenced to four years in prison.

In the immediate aftermath of the Comet Ping Pong shooting, some platforms did try banning the hashtag Pizzagate. But the underlying conspiracy theory just morphed into something else – as a part of the sprawling web of delusions and conspiracy theories that would become QAnon.

Despite the revelations in the wake of the Comet Ping Pong shooting, there are still hundreds of thousands of Americans who believe that Hillary Clinton and other prominent Democrats are part of a global cabal of Satan worshippers who traffic in kidnapped children, who they use to perform ritual human sacrifice, cannibalize for their adrenochrome, or sexually abuse. Or some combination of all three. The various parts of this conspiracy theory are frequently repeated and alluded to by right-wing pundits as though they are just accepted truth.

People outside the right-wing media bubble are often shocked by these beliefs. They don't understand how anyone could believe such obviously ridiculous allegations. But just like with cult beliefs, they didn't start out with the crazy. The beliefs start small, with true – or at least, reasonable – claims. That claim is used as a steppingstone to another claim, slightly less credible, and so on, step by step, until before you know it, you've gone so far down the rabbit hole, you're living in an alternate reality.

If, like me, you've been listening to right-wingers smear the Clintons (and commit violent acts of terrorism against the left) since the 1980s, the Pizzagate allegations – while more unhinged and unbelievable – were just the next step of the same old allegations and conspiracy theories they'd been accusing the Clintons of for decades.

Pizzagate wasn't the first time these unhinged anti-Clinton conspiracy theories – concocted and spread by right-wing lunatics – bled into the real world, with tragic consequences.

And sadly, it wouldn't be the last.

ENDNOTES:

1. Core, "Comet Ping Pong," https://coredc.com/projects/comet-ping-pong#/info/153

2. "Farm to Table," *Diners, Drive-Ins, and Dives*, Season 9, Episode 9, aired June 27, 2010. Food Network.

3. Cometpingpong.com, archived on the Wayback Machine at https://web.archive.org/web/20131204145450/http://www.cometpingpong.com/

4. Linda Wertheimer, "Fake News Surge Pins D.C. Pizzeria As Home To Child Trafficking," *NPR's Morning Edition*, aired November 27, 2016.

5. Wertheimer, "Fake News Surge."

6. Amanda Robb, "Anatomy of a Fake News Scandal," *Rolling Stone*, November 16, 2017.

7. Robb, "Anatomy."

8. Robb, "Anatomy."

9. Robb, "Anatomy."

10. "The saga of 'Pizzagate': The fake story that shows how conspiracy theories spread," *BBC Trending*, December 2, 2016.

11. Robb, "Anatomy."

12. Robb, "Anatomy."

13. Robb, "Anatomy."

14. Robb, "Anatomy."

15. Marc Fisher, John Woodrow Cox, and Peter Hermann, "Pizzagate: From rumor, to hashtag, to gunfire in D.C.," *The Washington Post*, December 6, 2016.

16. Robb, "Anatomy."

17. Michelle E. Miller, "The Pizzagate gunman is out of prison. Conspiracy theories are out of control," *The Seattle Times*, February 6, 2021.

18. Miller, "Pizzagate gunman."

19. Miller, "Pizzagate gunman."

20. *Mute*. Kathy Sue Holtorf, director. Edgar Maddison Welch, writer. 2011. YouTube, 8:40.

21. Fisher, Cox, and Hermann, "Pizzagate."

22. Miller, "Pizzagate gunman."

23. Miller, "Pizzagate gunman."

24. Miller, "Pizzagate gunman."

25. Fisher, Cox, and Hermann, "Pizzagate."

26. Fisher, Cox, and Hermann, "Pizzagate."

27. Adam Goldman, "Ping Pong Gunman Answers Our Reporter's Questions," *New York Times*, December 7, 2016.

28. WUSA9, "Raw: 'Pizzagate' suspect records message to his family on way to DC," posted June 22, 2017. YouTube, 1:44.

29. BBC News, "Trump aide Michael Flynn Jnr out after 'Pizzagate' tweets," December 7, 2016.

PART I

Chapter 1: A Small-Town Crime

The America of 1984, at least the one portrayed on TV, was big, shiny, loud, and triumphant. Ronald Reagan was running for re-election – and would win – on the slogan, "It's morning in America." Songs like "Girls Just Wanna Have Fun," "Let's Go Crazy," and "Jump" expressed the totally stoked, party-hard vibe of the time.

But underneath that slick, dazzling veneer of the mid-'80s, a lot of Americans were suffering. During the previous four years, tens of thousands of auto workers and other related industries had faced layoffs and plant closures. The Satanic Panic was in full swing. HIV had been identified as the cause of AIDS, but it would be another year before Reagan would even acknowledge its existence. And the Cold War was still very much a thing.

While the competing forces of optimism and fear duked it out in the wider country, Forrest City, Arkansas, seemed like a world away. In this small town in the southeastern part of a small state, 1984 was still a lot like the 1970s.

It's important – and relevant – to point out that the name, "Forrest City," isn't spelled that way because its founders were illiterate. The town is named after one of its founders, the notorious slave trader, Confederate general, and one of the first leaders of the KKK, Nathan Bedford Forrest. In this town, his legacy was still alive and well in the mid-'80s. Despite the fact that nearly half of Forrest City residents were African American, a racially integrated prom would still be four years away – and afterwards, in retaliation, the public school system would cancel all school-sponsored dances and social activities for years afterwards.

But things weren't all bad. The Japanese electronics firm Sanyo had recently opened a TV manufacturing plant in the city, giving it an economic boost. While the company had good relations with the local union and paid its workers a fair wage (at that point, anyway), the majority of the city's residents still lived below the poverty line.

But not the Stevens family. Walter Stevens III – known just as "Stevie" – ran a successful funeral home. Like most funeral homes at the time, it had been a family-run business, and Stevie was the fourth generation of Stevenses to run it. That made the Stevenses old money, and definitely one of the most prominent families of Forrest City.

Stevie was also a distant cousin, and political donor, to then-governor Bill Clinton – a fact that would eventually eclipse all the other facts about this story.

In 1984, Stevie's older daughter, Sara Ashley, who went by Ashley, was seventeen years old and a cheerleader at Forrest City High School.

On the afternoon of September 11, she got out of school at about two thirty and walked home, stopping by the Diamond Burger for a Coke on the way. The trip, she estimated, took about ten minutes.

While a lot of kids in the '80s came home to an empty house after school, Ashley usually didn't. But this was a Tuesday, the one day of the week her stepmother, Lisa, worked outside the home.

Once there, she walked through the unlocked door – this was a safe neighborhood, after all – and kicked off her shoes. As she told the *Kansas City Star*: "It was any old afternoon after school, and I was half doing homework, half watching television, and mostly waiting for some friends to come by."[1]

Only minutes after she arrived, a thin man with a scraggly beard and piercing blue eyes walked in through the side door. He had a paper bag in one hand and a pistol in the other. She said he tied her hands behind her back and asked her where her car keys were. She told him, and he forced her at gunpoint to get into her car.

He made her lie down in the seat and drove her to a nearby secluded area, the gun pointed at her the entire time. But Ashley had lived in Forrest City long enough to know exactly where he was going, right down to the streets: down McCollum to Cranor, then left on Cranor to the highway, where he turned right to Lindsuer, where he took a right again, then another right onto Virginia Circle.

"He drove up as far as Dr. Wollum's second driveway," she later told police. But then he pulled into the driveway, turned around, and drove back towards Lindseur, as though he had passed a specific spot and needed to go back to it. Back on Lindseur, Ashley said, he then turned off onto the first gravel road on the left. "He drove down this road a little way," she said, "and then turned off to the left behind some trees."

Once there, he got out, took her by the arm, and pulled her out of the car. He led her down a path a little way to a spot where he declared, "This will do," and set her down on the ground.

He took off her jeans and underwear and placed them under her, then took a butcher knife out of the paper sack. "Don't worry," he said to her, "I am not going to hurt you."

He used the knife to cut her sweater up the middle, and down both sleeves, nicking her shoulder in the process. Then he cut her bra off.

He asked her how old she was. She told him, "Sixteen," hoping to play on his sympathy. He then took a roll of tape out of the bag and used it to tape her mouth shut before taking off his jeans.

He asked her if she'd ever heard of a French tickler, but since her mouth was taped shut, she couldn't answer.

He put on the condom and tried to rape her vaginally. When he couldn't manage that, he said, "You're going to have to help me." He took the condom off and forced her to perform oral sex on him, threatening her, "If you bite me, I'll kill you."

He ejaculated in her mouth. She spit it out, and some of that spit ended up on her jeans, which were on the ground.

After that, he briefly penetrated her vaginally.

When he was done, Ashley asked him what he wanted now. He said, "Your life." When she asked him why, he said, "Because you can identify me."

She begged for her life, claiming her mom had cancer, again trying to play on his sympathies.

It must have worked, because he allowed her to get dressed and get back in the car. As he was trying to pull away, though, he had trouble getting the car out of the muddy spot where he'd parked. She said he tried to back up, but couldn't, just spinning the tires on the grass. So instead, he drove forward around a large tree and through some bushes.

The man drove her home, the entire time threatening her that if she told anyone about what happened, he would kill her.

Ashley then watched him get into his truck – a red Ford with a missing tailgate and a broken right headlight – and drive off. The time was approximately three twenty-five.

Ashley said once she was home, she took a shower – a common instinct for sexual assault victims. Then she called the cops. Forrest City Police Sgt. Bill Dooley was the initial investigator on her case.

She was able to describe her attacker clearly, especially his big "crystal blue" eyes, as well as the gun he'd threatened her with. She gave detailed directions to where he had driven with her, leading the police to the spot where she'd been raped.

There, the police found an area in the grass that had been disturbed, as though a struggle had taken place. There was a roll of packing tape on the ground, as well as fresh tire tracks in the grass, which appeared to corroborate her statement.

The Forrest City Police officers who responded undoubtedly knew who Ashley Stevens' dad was. Unlike many rape victims, the daughter of a well-to-do family was simply believed, so they didn't feel the need to take tire impressions or crime scene photos, or even question the neighbors or potential witnesses.

Back at the station, she was shown multiple lineups, but she couldn't positively pick her attacker out of any of them. One fellow fit the description of her attacker, but she didn't think it was him.

Despite not doing most of the basic evidence gathering, the police did do two things right: they took fingerprints from her car and samples of what they assumed to be semen from her jeans and underwear. The fingerprints ended up being unusable.

The biological samples, however, would prove to be more useful.

Six weeks went by without a suspect in her case.

Until one late October day, when she was riding in a friend's car downtown. When they slowed down at an intersection, "I looked over and there he was," she said. "We were turning left, waiting for the traffic to go by, and he passed us on the right."[2]

Ashley saw her attacker driving by in a red Ford pick-up truck, just like the one she had seen driving away on the day of her attack (though now, the tailgate had been replaced). Her friend wrote down the license plate number, and they both went back to the police with this new information.

Using the registration information on the truck, police were able to identify her attacker as Wayne Eugene Dumond.

***

Wayne was born and raised in the small town of DeWitt, Arkansas, about an hour and a half southwest of Forrest City.

DeWitt was never a big city, but when Wayne was born, in 1949, it was on the upswing. Like most towns in the Arkansas Delta, DeWitt's fortunes were tied to agriculture, and rice specifically; it was a center for rice milling and processing. Those were the kinds of jobs that paid better than farmwork, so while it was still poor, DeWitt was a little more prosperous than the surrounding towns.[3]

Wayne was the second of two sons born to Ira Eugene and Ethel Christine Dumond – both of whom went by their middle names. (Note: some sources spell the name "DuMond," but Wayne himself didn't capitalize the M).

Tragedy struck when his mother died in 1956. She was just shy of her thirtieth birthday; Wayne was only seven years old.

His father remarried rather quickly, and his sons did not take well to their new stepmother. Wayne said he hated her.

According to Wayne, he became a "hell-raiser" soon afterwards.

In high school, he was known around DeWitt as trouble: a heavy drinker and druggie who cruised around town with his no-account friends in an orange van. As one woman said, "Anyone with good sense knew to stay away when they saw that van."[4] One woman who lived in DeWitt at the same time as Wayne said that he raped her friend's sister when they were in high school. But like so many sexual assault victims, she chose not to report it to the authorities, though she did tell her sister and close friends at the time. As part of those conversations, it was alleged that he'd done the same to other girls in town.[5]

According to Wayne, he enlisted in the Army in 1967 because he figured he'd be drafted anyway. According to records, he was actually drafted.

Sometime in 1968, before he was shipped off to Vietnam, he married his first wife, Lywanda Jean Strain.

While he was in the Army, as he told author Guy Reel, he was a "good soldier," but continued to drink heavily and do drugs.[6] He claimed it was when he got back from his tour of duty that he started doing harder drugs like acid and PCP.

It's also when he would tell a peculiar story to anyone who'd listen. He told folks that he and his unit had come across a village in Cambodia that wasn't on the map. So, he said, they "corrected the map" by killing every living thing and burning it to the ground. The folks in DeWitt who heard him tell this story say that he didn't show any emotion when he spoke about it. In fact, they say, he sounded like he was bragging about it.[7]

Now, we don't have any evidence that this happened, and we know Wayne only had a passing relationship to the truth. But even if it was a lie, it does say something about his character that he would brag about something like that.

He hadn't been back stateside for long when he was arrested in Lawton, Oklahoma, near Fort Sill, in the summer of 1972. Wayne and two other men were charged with murder.

It seems the victim – a fellow soldier – was dating the ex-wife of a man named Bill Cherry, which Cherry wasn't so happy about. So Bill got his seventeen-year-old daughter to lure the victim to a secluded area, where he, Wayne, and a third man beat the man to death with claw hammers and pipes.

But Wayne knew the old adage, "the first one to squeal gets the deal." In exchange for testifying against his accomplices, all charges against him were dropped.

The next year, 1973, he was stationed in Tacoma, Washington, when he was arrested for assaulting an eighteen-year-old woman in a mall parking lot. He claimed the woman had almost run him over, so he had only "shown" her the knife he'd been carrying.

The woman told a very different story: she said he grabbed her, held a knife to her throat, and demanded she get into his vehicle. But she screamed and fought back, so she was able to escape.

At first, he skipped out on his bond and went AWOL, but later came back and turned himself in. He was convicted of second-degree assault and was sentenced to five years – deferred – and mandatory counseling. During that court-ordered counseling, Wayne was diagnosed as "mildly schizoid" with "an inferiority complex and a need to prove his masculinity."

This conviction apparently put an end to his military career. So Wayne came back to DeWitt.

And, from the outside, it seemed like Lywanda had finally gotten him to settle down. They built a house on an acre of land his father gave them, and the couple had three boys before Wayne got a vasectomy through the V.A.

They went to church every Sunday. But every other day of the week, Wayne drank heavily, and at some point, started growing weed.

He was going back to some of his other old habits, too. Sometime in 1976, he forced his way into the house of one of their neighbors, a twenty-two-year-old woman who was also an old schoolmate of his. She said he held her at knifepoint, threatening to kill her three-year-old daughter, who was sleeping in the bed next to her, if she screamed. She said she was so afraid of him hurting her daughter that she stayed silent, stroking her daughter's hair to keep her from waking, while Wayne raped her.

The woman was terrified of Wayne – after all, she'd known him from high school – and out of fear, didn't report the rape until over a month later.

When questioned by the police, Wayne claimed he was drunk and stoned and didn't remember anything – not exactly a full-throated denial. Years later, he would change his story and say that at the time, he had been selling drugs. He claimed the victim couldn't pay him and so asked him if she could "take it out in trade," and he agreed. "The next thing I know, she was yelling rape," he said.[8]

Since the woman declined to testify against him, the charges were dropped on the condition that he undergo counseling. There's no evidence that he ever underwent that counseling.

Later that year, he was accused of another attempted rape, this time in Little Rock. Once again, he entered the victim's house wielding a butcher knife and threatening her. But as soon as he saw her boyfriend lying in the bed next to her, he took off.

The woman reported it, but the police discouraged her from pressing charges. Since there wasn't any evidence of a crime, it would be next to impossible to prosecute, they told her.

It's not clear exactly when Lywanda left Wayne, but it had to have been not long after two separate women accused him of rape. The couple officially divorced in 1980, and Wayne kept custody of their three sons.

Wayne said he wanted a fresh start, so he took the boys and moved away from DeWitt. They moved into a small house in the woods outside Forrest City, in rural St. Francis County. There, Wayne worked a string of odd jobs: mechanic, maintenance man, construction laborer. None of which he could hold down for long, thanks to his drinking.

Three years after he moved to Forrest City, another woman entered Wayne's life – this time, by walking right up to his front door.

Mary Lou Wolf – who went by "Dusty" – was a petite brunette, standing just over five feet tall, though her curly hairstyle added a few inches. Her small face was nearly lost behind large, rimless glasses that went out of style a decade earlier.

Dusty was a church-going woman, but she had a pretty checkered past. In March 1983, when she knocked on Wayne's door with a chocolate pie and a pot of stew, she was still in the middle of divorce proceedings from her fifth or sixth husband, depending on how you want to count them.

By May, Dusty and Wayne were married, and she moved herself and her fourteen-year-old daughter, Jinger, in with Wayne and his sons.

***

November 1, 1984, was just five days before Election Day, when Ronald Reagan would be re-elected to the presidency, and Bill Clinton would be re-elected as governor of Arkansas for his third, non-consecutive, term. St. Francis County would also re-elect its sheriff, Coolidge Conlee.

On that unseasonably warm Thursday, Wayne was alone at home, shirtless, a whiskey and Coke in hand, when officers arrived to take him in for questioning in the kidnapping and rape of Ashley Stevens.[9]

He was put into a lineup for Ashley to pick out. Even though Wayne had shaved since the last time she'd seen him, Ashley recognized him immediately. It was his "crystal blue eyes."

Wayne was arrested and charged with rape and kidnapping. He – or, more likely, Dusty – posted his $75,000 bond and went back home.

While he was awaiting trial, something terrible happened, though exactly what depends on who's telling the tale.

ENDNOTES:

1. Matt Stearns, "Rumors shroud suspect's record," *The Kansas City Star*, July 1, 2001. p. A1.

2. Stearns, "Rumors," p. A1.

3. Bryce Keaton, "Fake News Killed Carol Sue Shields," YouTube, 29:42. January 22, 2018.

4. Keaton, "Fake News."

5. Keaton, "Fake News."

6. Guy Reel, *Unequal Justice: Wayne Dumond, Bill Clinton, and the Politics of Rape in Arkansas,* (Buffalo, New York: Prometheus Books, 1993), p. 28.

7. Keaton, "Fake News."

8. Joe Farmer, "Parole board hears Dumond's side," *Arkansas Democrat*, September 13, 1990.

9. Reel, *Unequal Justice*, pp. 16-17.

Chapter 2: Coolidge Conlee and Wayne Dumond's Testicles

March 7, 1985, was a Thursday. Wayne's two younger sons, eleven-year-old Michael and nine-year-old Joey, rode the bus home from school, then walked up the long gravel driveway to their house.

Once they stepped through the door, they encountered something out of a nightmare. Their dad was lying on their kitchen floor, barely conscious, with twine wrapped around his wrists and ankles. A huge pool of blood was spreading beneath him. His severed testicles were lying on the floor nearby.

In his statement to Arkansas State Police Lt. Phil Osterman a few days later, Wayne gave his first account of what happened.

According to this, his original statement, between one thirty and one forty-five that afternoon, "I had just come back from my mailbox up on the paved road. I was in the kitchen putting up some dishes and two men came in the unlocked front door.

"There were two of them, a short one, five-foot-nine or so and about 150 pounds. He had a .38 caliber revolver, blue, with about a four-inch barrel. It had brown grips, probably plastic. He was wearing a blue and brown plaid shirt, blue jeans, and old high top work shoes. Both of the men had on stocking mask[s] and blue green rubber gloves, not surgical gloves because they fit too loose.

"The tall one was about six foot two or six foot three. He was medium built, about 180 or 190 pounds. They pointed the gun at me and motioned for me to lay down on the floor. They tied my hands behind my back and my feet together, then tied my hands and my feet all together behind me. I thought they were going to shoot me.

"I was on my side, and the small one put one knee on my shoulder and the gun to the side of my head. The big one pulled my pants down. He had a knife in his hand when he came in. The blade was about four inches long. It looked like stainless steel. The hand guard was stainless steel or chrome. As he cut on me I blacked out for a little while. I was screaming and hollering and don't remember too much.

"As they were leaving, the small one said, 'good job.' The other one said, 'Mr. C will be proud.'"[1]

Wayne told Lt. Osterman that he didn't recognize either of the men, but noted that about a week before that, he had noticed a little red car parked on his driveway with no one around it.[2]

When the boys came home to find their dad in this state, Michael helped him cut off his bindings, and Joey ran to a neighbors to call for help. They sent an ambulance, and, since this was an apparent assault, they sent the law as well. And the top law enforcement official in St. Francis County in 1985 was Sheriff Coolidge Conlee.

He arrived on the scene after Lt. Ostermann, passing the ambulance as it sped towards the hospital. He walked into a house that looked like an abattoir, with blood and tissue underfoot. But as Ostermann left the scene to follow the ambulance to the hospital, Conlee waded into it. He first picked up a blood-soaked bit of twine – no doubt cut off of Wayne – then dropped it. Then he spotted two pink globs of tissue – Wayne's severed testicles.

Conlee immediately scooped them up into a matchbox and left the scene.

A wiry, "bantam sized" man who walked with a swagger and chain-smoked Kools, Coolidge Conlee had been operating outside the law since at least 1954, when he'd been convicted of illegal gambling in Tennessee. By 1960, he'd racked up four federal charges of tax evasion. He pled guilty and got off with a fine and a year of probation.[3]

In the 1960s, Conlee was spending a lot of time in Hot Springs, Arkansas, a town known as much for its mob ties as its bathhouses. He was well known for chasing women, shooting craps, and running illegal gambling houses. In particular, he would come into Hot Springs during the horse races, specifically to steer wealthy folks away from the tracks and into his illegal floating dice games on nearby Lake Hamilton.

In one illegal gambling house where he was acting as pit boss -- this one operating out of the historic Ohio Club -- an FBI raid found him in possession of marked cards and shaved dice.[4]

But in what would become a pattern, despite all the evidence against him, he was acquitted.

His shady reputation notwithstanding, he landed his first political position on the Forrest City school board – as a pro-segregation candidate. He would go on to win every single election he ran in.

In 1972, he won a seat on the Forrest City city council in a landslide. At the same time, he was serving as president of the board of the all-white Nathan Bedford Forrest Academy, one of the many private, all-white schools that cropped up after the Supreme Court struck down segregation in public schools.

Two years later, he was elected mayor by campaigning that he would be "an honest mayor." It was in this race that his past criminality came up – but while he admitted he'd been "involved in gambling" in his past, he'd "sought forgiveness from God and been given guidance."[5]

Apparently, the voters bought it. He won that race handily, and his first act as mayor was to abolish the Civil Service Commission – giving him free reign to appoint whoever he wanted to head the various civil service agencies, such as the fire and police departments. And he did just that, appointing his associate Joe Goff as chief of police.

In 1980, he ran for sheriff of St. Francis County and won – probably thanks to having uniformed police officers threaten Black folks at polling stations and running bootlegged liquor to Black-owned businesses on Election Day.[6]

Within a couple months of taking office, he was apparently back to his old ways, shooting craps with his deputies in high-stakes games right in the sheriff's office – and using weighted dice.

But he was up to more than just cheating at some backroom gambling. Conlee was running the county like a mafia don. The mayor of Forrest City at the time, Danny Ferguson, had been Conlee's administrative assistant when he was mayor. The county elections commissioner, Dora Hughes, was the wife of Conlee's deputy Sambo Hughes (and served on the county's Democratic Central Committee).[7]

Even the district legal authorities were in his pocket: circuit judge John Anderson and district prosecuting attorney, Gene Raff, were known to shoot dice with Conlee; Raff's assistant, Fletcher Long, acted as Conlee's personal attorney. They were all known to gamble and shoot dice with Conlee at his businesses and other places around town – including at Stevens Funeral Home. In fact, Raff, Long, and Stevens had all been brothers in the Kappa Sigma Fraternity at the University of Arkansas in the early 1960s.

With every legal official from the city police chief to the circuit judge in his pocket, Conlee enjoyed almost total immunity. He and his deputies, Sambo Hughes and Larry Henley, ran illegal liquor stores and gambling houses, extorted Black-owned businesses for protection, and solicited bribes in exchange for dropping charges or even to retrieve stolen property. They would also regularly threaten witnesses and beat prisoners in custody.

They also had a pretty lucrative little side hustle selling confiscated drugs right out of the sheriff's office. After Conlee's election as sheriff, the chief of police of nearby Palestine, Luther Pitman, said that 150 pounds of "Colombian gold grass" had gone missing from the county courthouse. The "grass" had been confiscated in a highly publicized drug raid, where Conlee busted dozens of people. Yet, of the dozens of people arrested, only a few of them ever faced any charges. And apparently no effort was made to investigate where the marijuana had come from.

Later, a confidential informant working for the Arkansas State Police was arrested by Conlee's deputies for possessing drugs and explosives. When they saw papers in his wallet with state police investigators' names and numbers on them, they took the man out to a field, pulled out a 30-30 shotgun, and pointed it at his chest. They threatened him that if he worked with the state police, he'd be killed, and that they could get it done for $200. They then told the man to get out of town.

But despite sworn statements from witnesses, incriminating evidence on tape, and lab results showing the marijuana he was selling was that same "Colombian gold" that had gone missing from the county courthouse, the local police (headed by Conlee's appointee, Joe Goff) refused to investigate. The Arkansas State Police forwarded their investigation to District Attorney Gene Raff, who likewise refused to prosecute the case.

So Conlee wasn't just boasting when he told a reporter, "I run this county." He was making a statement of fact.

And it was just this swaggering hubris that is to thank for the most well-known – and bizarre – fact about this case. Because Wayne Dumond's testicles never made their way into any evidence locker. Instead, Conlee kept them in his office, preserved in a jar of formaldehyde, for quite some time. He would take them out and brag to anyone who asked: "This is what happens when you rape a cheerleader in my county," before, eventually, flushing them down the toilet in front of a reporter.

But the stench of Conlee's criminality and corruption was starting to waft further than the borders of St. Francis County. Enter Jack Hill, a reporter for KAIT in Jonesboro, Arkansas, who had recently begun looking into a suspicious fire at Conlee's crop-dusting business.

ENDNOTES:

1. Phil Osterman, "Interview of Victim, File Number: 52-215-85" (Arkansas State Police Criminal Investigation Division, Little Rock, Arkansas, March 19, 1985). p. 1.

2. Osterman, "Interview of Victim," p. 2.

3. Jack Hill, producer. "I Run This County," KAIT, aired February 11, 1985.

4. Hill, "I Run This County."

5. Jack E. Hill, "Wins on Stump, Records Citing Days as Gambler Precede New Conlee Bid," *Arkansas Democrat*, April 27, 1986. p. 26.

6. Hill, "I Run This County."

7. Hill, "Wins on Stump," p. 27.

Chapter 3: Jack Hill, Reporting For Arkansas

Jack Hill began his reporting on St. Francis County in 1984, investigating racial discrimination against Black farmers. As he was riding around the county with a resident, the woman pointed out a sheriff's car, and told Jack that Sheriff Conlee was involved in gambling, bootlegging, and drug dealing. "I'm afraid of him," she said.[1]

That was all it took to turn on Jack's reporter's instincts. Corruption had been his beat since 1970, with his very first investigative feature. In it, he exposed the problems with low-income housing in the state of Mississippi. That feature would go on to be nominated for an Emmy.

Often described as a "straight arrow," Jack had enjoyed an idyllic, "All American" childhood.

He was born in Rogers, in the northwest corner of Arkansas, in 1940, the only child of a war veteran father and schoolteacher mother. He showed himself to be an overachiever even in high school: class president, Honor Society member, star basketball player, voted Most Likely to Succeed.

And this was where his interest in broadcast journalism first emerged. While still a student, he worked with a local radio station, hosting a Saturday-afternoon program focused on Rogers High School.

He went on to study speech (what we might now call communications or rhetoric) at the University of Arkansas, just down the road from Rogers, in Fayetteville. There, he was inducted into the ROTC's honor society and served as chaplain for his fraternity. He was even featured in the local papers as a hero for rescuing a kid while he was working as a lifeguard one summer. And, of course, he interned with a local television station.

After earning his degree in 1962, he served in the Army for two years before being honorably discharged. He immediately went back to school and earned his master's in broadcast journalism – funded by a generous William Gregory Fellowship – from the University of Missouri.

After a brief stint at a station in Denver, he went on to a station in Jackson, Mississippi, where he produced "Homes Like These," his Emmy-nominated piece about the low-income housing crisis.

He also met Anne Powers there, and in August of 1973, the two were married.

Jack would move on again after that, to a station in Dallas, briefly, before eventually landing an anchor position with KAIT in Jonesboro, in northeast Arkansas, in 1975.

Tall, dark-haired, with a deep authoritative voice, it didn't take long for Jack to become "a local Walter Cronkite, measured and reserved in manner, projecting a fair-minded respect for both his material and his audience..."[2]

There was one notable exception to that, and it's the place where Jack Hill first intersected with this story, though unwittingly.

In 1979, Jack interviewed the state's new first lady, Hillary Rodham, on his weekly public affairs program, *In Focus*. That interview planted some of the first seeds of anti-Hillary sentiment in the state. But we'll get into that later.

When he wasn't behind the anchor desk or interviewing local bigwigs on *In Focus*, Jack was working with a small team producing hard-hitting investigative pieces on slum housing, the conditions in the county jail, railroad crossing safety, and – importantly – corruption. All of which went on to earn him and KAIT numerous awards, including another Emmy nomination.

So when he heard that Sheriff Conlee was apparently engaging in a number of illegal operations, he dove into the story with the same zeal he brought to all his work.

Jack found people willing to talk – anonymously – about Conlee's many illegal activities. And one very suspicious fire.

During the time Conlee had held his various elected offices, he also ran several businesses: Forrest City Asphalt, C&G Car Sales, and Forrest City Aviation, along with some liquor stores.

In the early morning hours of February 17, 1984, the hangar at Forrest City Aviation caught fire. Twice. And Conlee collected a $700,000 insurance payout to reimburse him for the loss.

That would have been the end of it, but sometime later, Conlee's son Kenneth was caught selling radios that had supposedly been destroyed in the fire, which Conlee had collected insurance reimbursement for. The father and son were both charged with insurance fraud.

In the well-established pattern of lenience that Conlee enjoyed, the charges against both him and Kenneth were greatly reduced, and the two were allowed to plea down to lesser charges, pay $1,700 in restitution, and walk free.

So Jack started asking questions.

The facts of the case alone raised red flags: the first fire, which was called in to the fire department at 3:33 a.m., was small and fully extinguished in minutes. It caused only minor smoke damage.

Then, at 4:33 a.m. – only minutes after the firefighters had cleared the scene and left – another fire was called in. This one was much larger and hotter. It burned Forrest City Aviation to the ground.

This raised all kinds of alarms (the metaphorical kind) for the captain of the fire department, since the first blaze had been so small and completely extinguished when the firefighters cleared the scene.

If there had somehow been smoking embers left behind, it would have taken anywhere from a half hour to four hours, or even days, for them to generate enough heat to have ignited the second fire.[3]

Adding to his suspicions, the captain of the fire department told Jack that while he was investigating the fire, he had gotten threatening phone calls.

Jack dug further. And he found quite a bit wrong with the Forrest City Aviation fire. According to multiple sources, Conlee didn't know how to run a legit business, and Forrest City Aviation was deeply in debt.[4]

Jack spoke to an employee who said that he had heard Conlee on the phone with Kenneth a couple of weeks before the fire, discussing in great detail about their fire insurance, including a statement that, "there might be a fire" there.[5]

Then Bruce Hayes, a pilot who rented hangar space in the building, told Jack that Kenneth Conlee had made him move his plane out of the hangar right before the fire. "He said that if the hangar should burn, that they didn't want to be liable," Hayes said. "They [Coolidge and Kenneth] were rather blunt that they definitely wanted the plane out by Thursday night, and, of course, by daylight Saturday morning, it [Forrest City Aviation] was in ashes."[6]

Jack also learned from a source who wished to remain anonymous that the two guard dogs that were usually kept on the property had been taken away before the fire as well.

Then, he uncovered the smoking gun (so to speak): the night before the fire, Conlee's deputy Sambo Hughes had purchased eight quarts of charcoal lighter fluid – the perfect accelerant, according to arson investigators, because it's hard to detect and evaporates quickly.

And, according to witnesses, Sambo had been on the scene at both fires.

***

On February 11, 1985, KAIT aired the first of ten reports on Coolidge Conlee, titled "I Run This County." In the report, Jack exposed Conlee's shady past, as well as the facts surrounding the fires at his crop-dusting business.

Jack's reports set off a ripple effect across the state. At one otherwise standard press conference, then-Governor Bill Clinton was asked if law enforcement was going to do anything about Coolidge Conlee's corruption. Clinton's reply was, "I haven't heard anything about it."

Jack heard this answer and took that as a challenge. He fired off a letter to Clinton detailing all the criminal activities he had uncovered, along with the web of corrupt officials who had covered it up. So, in a move that would later be lost down the media's memory hole, Clinton immediately ordered a probe into the allegations.

But in the meantime, Jack's investigation put him and his sources – including law enforcement officers – at great risk.

Shortly after the series aired, Arkansas State Police troopers living in Forrest City were subjected to a campaign of harassment. They would find their yards littered with garbage, their cars "tampered with." One officer reported that in the early morning hours of February 28, someone attempted to break into his home. The officer fired his weapon, and the suspect fled.

Then on March 17 – just days after the Quorum Court, as requested by Governor Clinton, ordered an investigation into Conlee's corruption – there was another break-in. This time, again in the early hours, the intruder broke into an officer's home in south Forrest City. He went into the officer's six-year-old daughter's room and cut her underwear. The officer chased him off, and the intruder fled in the officer's personal car. He was, fortunately, apprehended immediately.

Yet Forrest City Police Chief Joe Goff insisted that these incidents weren't related.[7]

But let's back up to March 7, amid all this, when Wayne Dumond had been attacked and castrated at his home outside of Forrest City.

After the castration, Wayne had been rushed to the local hospital, then air-lifted to the Elvis Presley Trauma Center in Memphis. Oddly, Lt. Ostermann recalled hearing Dusty ask the attending doctor if he thought the castration had been self-inflicted. Since the doctor didn't have any knowledge of the crime scene – where Wayne had been tied up, and where there had been no weapon found – he said he couldn't rule it out. Later, when he was on the stand, he said he had seen rapists do this exact thing before, either as a ploy for mercy or a misguided attempt to remove the "problem."

After he was released from the hospital, Wayne and his family felt they weren't safe, and the law certainly wouldn't protect them. Wayne and Dusty sent the kids to live with other family members, and the two of them stayed with Wayne's family back in DeWitt.

But even though they were in hiding, they weren't laying low – at least Dusty wasn't.

It's hard to overestimate just how much of a force Dusty was for Wayne's cause. As soon as Wayne was arrested, she had leapt to his defense. She wrote to Stevie Stevens personally to "explain" how it couldn't have been Wayne who raped his daughter, and included a photo of their family in the letter.[8] The day before the attack, she had testified to her church – Second Baptist – about how hard this had been on their family, and asked for their prayers.[9]

Just days after the attack, she called Ashley Stevens on the phone to try and convince her that she was "mistaken" about who had raped her.[10]

She embarked on a letter-writing campaign to Evangelical churches and other "fellow Christians." In her letters, sprinkled with pious exclamations of "praise God," "God bless you," and signing off, "In Christ's Love," she insists that Wayne is innocent, a good Christian man who was framed for a crime he didn't commit, and worse, mutilated, likely on the orders of corrupt Sheriff Conlee. She was able to convince some of those "fellow Christians" to also write to newspapers and Governor Clinton on Wayne's behalf.

Her letters to the editor and to legal officials, however, take a decidedly different tone. In one letter to the editor dated September 20, 1985, she talks about women who make false rape allegations: "These females, so-called because lady does not fit them, can ruin a person's life by a mistake like that..." She claims that the jurors only convicted her husband because they, too, feared being castrated or having their houses burned down, "All because this so-called victim was Gov. Clinton's cousin."

She concludes her letter, "I advise them to laugh and enjoy their sweet victory now, because hell lasts forever and 100 years here on earth is fleeting in comparison.

"I pray for you, all of you especially that have hurt my children and mutilated my husband and broken up our God-given family."

During that time, Dusty had, no doubt, seen "I Run This County," and surely thought that Jack would make a good ally in her crusade to exonerate her husband. She called him at the news station right after Wayne's castration. "I can't tell you who I am," she said, "But a man was castrated today near Forrest City. You may have heard of him. His name is Wayne Dumond. He's been charged with rape and was awaiting trial. I just thought you'd want to know."[11]

Then in mid-March – less than two weeks later – Dusty wrote to Jack to personally plead Wayne's case. In her letter, she tells Jack that Wayne "gave his life to Christ" in 1978, and that he was a "model husband."[12]

Knowing all he did about Conlee, including the fact that he was showing off Wayne's severed testicles, Jack quite reasonably suspected that Conlee at least knew what happened, and maybe even had something to do with it. So Jack agreed to look into it, and Anne agreed to help, touching off what would become a decades-long relationship with the Dumonds.

The police investigation into the attack, however, had seemed to stall out, with Conlee claiming he could find no leads. "Really, we just started from scratch," Conlee told a UPI reporter. "No clues. Not anything."[13] It didn't take long for Conlee to conclude that – despite what the evidence indicated – Wayne had done it to himself.

But even though Conlee claimed that he'd interviewed over 150 people, the case file showed that only three people were questioned by the sheriff's office, and the last date of any investigative activity was dated March 12, 1985 – just three days after the attack.[14] Such a perfunctory investigation –

along with the lie covering it up – must have raised Jack's alarms.

Luckily, Jack had developed good relationships with the Arkansas State Police officers who he'd worked with while investigating Conlee's corruption. One of them was Detective Fred Odom.

Odom contacted Jack with information that Charlie Hickman, an inmate in the nearby Phillips County jail, had called him at the end of April. Hickman had been angling to make a deal to get out of jail, and claimed he knew who had been behind the castration. When Odom asked if it was Conlee, Hickman said "yes."

As Jack and Anne investigated further, they found several more sources with information that pointed at a criminal conspiracy – with Conlee at the center.

In May, a cellmate of Hickman's wrote a letter to Floyd French, a member of the Quorum Court, that said, "Charlie told me himself that he was hired by Conlee to castrate the Dumond guy."

At a later interview, the cellmate said that Hickman had told him that it was actually "the father" (i.e., Ashley's father) who had paid for it through Conlee. Hickman had told him that after they castrated Wayne, they had left him for dead, thinking he would bleed out.

The cellmate said Hickman was "scared to death," thinking Conlee or one of his deputies was going to come and take him out, and he wanted to get this info to Odom. A second cellmate corroborated this conversation.

According to multiple sources around town, Hickman had allegedly bragged that he and Larry "Pork Chops" Lewis had done the deed, and that it had all been arranged by Stevens and Conlee. Others witnessed Hickman flashing a lot of cash around that time, and when asked about it, said he'd gotten it for "cutting off someone's nuts." Hickman reportedly said that Stevens had paid him $5,000 (though others would say he paid Conlee $15,000) to have the deed done, and had even supplied the gloves and the knife – which he and Lewis had buried in a swampy area known as "the bottoms" after they were done.

There were several other facts that indicated that Conlee and Stevens were involved. One source told Jack that Stevens had told multiple people about the castration days before it happened. And Conlee's and Stevens' actions on the day of the attack raised red flags as well.

Much later, it would come out that on March 7, Conlee had been at home when he got a phone call to go to the Dumond home. Along the way, for whatever reason, he stopped at Stevens Funeral Home to pick up a jar. After Conlee scooped up Wayne's testicles, he returned to the funeral home to put them in formaldehyde to "preserve them as evidence."

Stevens, it would later be revealed, had been at a steak dinner with some friends that afternoon, until his wife showed up and told him that someone from the sheriff's office was looking for him. He had an employee drive him to the courthouse, but Conlee wasn't there, so Stevens had him drive to the funeral home. There, the employee said, he saw testicles in a jar.

Sometime later, Conlee dropped Stevens off back at the dinner party, where he talked with several people about Wayne's castration – which had not yet been reported in the news.[15]

But that information about Conlee's and Stevens' activities didn't come out until much later. So all the evidence Jack had came from unnamed sources – or William Hickman.

To make matters worse, when he was interviewed on the record, Hickman retracted everything. He claimed that what he'd said to Odom on that phone call wasn't true; he'd only said it because he wanted to get out of jail so badly. When asked about his bragging around town that he'd "cut someone's nuts off," Hickman said he'd just been joking.

Hickman's alibi was that he and Lewis had been out of town, driving for C&L Trucking until the day of Wayne's attack.

At his interview, Lewis repeated Hickman's claims that he'd just been joking around about castrating someone, and that on March 7, they had been driving for C&L on a run to New York.

But Jack did his homework, and came with receipts.

First, C&L Trucking had no records of Hickman being on that trip.

Second, Hickman had said he'd loaded the truck in Holtsville, but according to the logbook, it was loaded in Willboro – throwing his entire timeline off. They said they hadn't gotten back until that day, March 7, but the logbook showed them getting back to Forrest City on March 5 – two days before Wayne's attack.

In May 1985, Jack ran yet another story about Conlee, this time connecting him to Wayne's castration.

Meanwhile, Jack continued digging into Conlee's many other criminal activities. Even after a ten-part series, he felt there was still more crime and corruption to uncover.

On June 7, he and his camera operator, Manochehr Nourizadeh, were in a rural area of St. Francis County, less than a mile south of Forrest City. Jack had gotten a tip that there was some illegal gambling going on at someone's private home.

So Jack and Manochehr drove the Channel 8 station wagon down a dirt road to the house.

Down the road a piece from the house, Manochehr began filming. Here is what that film captured:

The shot opens on Jack holding a microphone, the rather unremarkable house in the background. Soon Jack is approached by a large man who would later be identified as Calvin Adams, the sheriff of a nearby county. Jack introduces himself and asks how Adams is doing.

"All right; you got a problem?" Adams responds.

"No, sir, I'm Jack Hill with Channel 8 television. Who are you?"

"It don't make no difference who you are," he says.

"What is your name?"

"None of your fucking business," Adams responds.

"We're here on a public road, observing you. You're on television."

"Don't make no difference," he says.

"Could you tell me what's going on inside the house?"

"Yeah, we're having a birthday party," Adams answers.

Jack tries more questions, until he finally asks, "Why don't you let us in there?"[15]

At that point, Adams snatches Jack's mic out of his hand and starts hitting him on the head and shoulders with it. Jack runs into the surrounding woods, and Adams chases after him. Manochehr continues filming.

But then Adams turns around to Manochehr, who has caught everything on film. Adams grabs the camera out of Manochehr's hands and smashes it, ending the film.

Manochehr managed to escape in the station's car and call for help – not from the police, for obvious reasons. He first drove to a house up the road, but no one was home, so he drove back into Forrest City to find a pay phone. All the while, he had two cars after him – one was flashing blue lights, to pull him over, but Manochehr was rightfully suspicious of any law enforcement in that county.

Once in town, Manochehr called KAIT. The station manager then called the state police, who sent a patrol car to escort him to their headquarters. That patrol car was driven by Fred Odom, their trusted friend. He had been the one blue-lighting Manochehr, but Manochehr had no way of knowing that, and after taking his statement, Odom understood why he didn't pull over.

After speaking with Manochehr, Odom drove out to the scene of the crime, where Jack was still hiding in the woods in fear for his life.

Jack said when he heard Odom's voice calling out for him, he knew it was finally safe to come out.

But Jack would soon be facing a threat even bigger than a corrupt, violent sheriff.

ENDNOTES:

1. Larry Cooper, "Crusading newsman draws nation's eye as corruption fight gets rough," *Northwest Arkansas Morning News*, January 13, 1989.

2. Dale Carpenter, and Robert Cochran, *Reporting for Arkansas: The Documentary Films of Jack Hill*, (Fayetteville, Arkansas: University of Arkansas Press, 2022), p. 64.

3. Jack Hill, producer. "I Run This County," KAIT, aired February 11, 1985.

4. Hill, "I Run This County."

5. Hill, "I Run This County."

6. Hill, "I Run This County."

7. "Incidents involving troopers not related, Chief Goff says," (Forrest City) *Times-Herald*, March 22, 1985.

8. Special Collections, Jack Hill papers, Series 3 Box 43, Folder 19.

9. Guy Reel, *Unequal Justice: Wayne Dumond, Bill Clinton, and the Politics of Rape in Arkansas* (Buffalo, New York: Prometheus Books, 1993), p. 37.

10. Hill papers, Series 3 Box 43, Folder 19.

11. Reel, *Unequal Justice*, pp. 60-61.

12. Hill papers, Series 3, Box 91, Folder 32.

13. "No leads in castration case," UPI, March 9, 1985.

14. Jack Hill, "'Knew' sheriff wasn't telling truth, Dumond's wife says," *Arkansas Democrat*, April 17, 1986.

15. Hill papers, Series 3, Box 43, Folder 19

16. "Jonesboro TV station says 2 on assignment hit, camera smashed," *Arkansas Gazette*, ~June 12, 1985.

Chapter 4: The (First) Conviction of Wayne Dumond – and the Downfall of Coolidge Conlee

Since the gruesome attack, the Dumond family had fled their home in fear. But Wayne and Dusty knew they couldn't just abandon their house – that would be like an open invitation to burglars or vandals. So Wayne would secretly drive up there a couple days a week to pick up the mail, mow the yard, and generally keep the place looking inhabited.

But that wasn't enough.

On or around July 10, 1985, the Dumonds' house caught fire. Because it was so rural, firefighters didn't get there until the fire was well underway, and the house burned to the ground. The fire marshall made the determination that the fire had started in the attic, probably from a faulty light switch, and ruled it was accidental.

No further investigation was conducted.

In August, Wayne stood trial for aggravated rape and kidnapping. Since Ashley had been a minor at the time of the attack, her name was left out of the reporting.

The trial almost seemed written for tabloid TV: a salacious sex crime, a corrupt Southern sheriff, and a violent castration. Though Guy Reel, then a reporter for the Memphis *Commercial Appeal*, had broken the story of

Wayne's castration, the story had quickly been picked up by the larger, national media, including the tabloid TV show *Inside Edition*.

But there was one reporter who was noticeably absent from the courtroom: Jack Hill.

The summer of 1985 had been a hard one on Jack. KAIT had been, like most media outlets at that time, a family-owned station. The owners, while certainly motivated to earn enough advertising revenue to keep the lights on, operated the station in the spirit of public service. But in what would become a pattern of consolidation that would, within a few decades, hollow out local newsrooms across the nation, KAIT was sold to a national media chain. The new owners saw the newsroom as little more than an asset, something to maximize profits above all else.

And, thanks to Jack's reporting, Conlee had filed a defamation suit against both Jack and the station. While it was clear that the suit had no chance of success, it still represented a potential loss of profits.

So, just days after Jack was attacked by Calvin Adams on that rural dirt road, the new management called him into the office. They wanted him to sign a contract – or more accurately, a list of demands. This new contract stipulated that he would never again report on anything in St. Francis County. In addition, he would not be allowed to step foot in the county – or even to call or receive a call from anyone there.

The new management gave him a choice: either sign the contract or resign. Jack, a dedicated journalist to the end, resigned.

Now unemployed, and with a defamation suit hanging over his head making him unemployable, Jack was desperately trying to find any way to support himself. He couldn't attend

Wayne's trial, but he did follow the news reports – splashed across the front page of most papers – every day.

The chief prosecutor on the case was, of course, Gene Raff, assisted by Fletcher Long. The bailiff for the courtroom was none other than Sheriff Conlee.

The judge on the case, Harvey Yates, made a ruling early on that Wayne's castration – as well as Sheriff Conlee's treatment of his severed testicles afterwards – and his house fire were not admissible in court, since those facts had nothing to do with the crime itself and would unfairly prejudice the jury in Wayne's favor.

The prosecution's opening statement laid the case out pretty simply: this is the man the victim said raped her. The serological evidence supported it.

Wayne's defense, which was being handled by Larry Horton from Malvern and Bill McArthur from Little Rock, was that this was a case of mistaken identity. He admitted that while he did leave work early that day, it was because he was sick, and he was at home, alone, the entire afternoon and evening. The defense also took aim at the serological evidence the state was using against him; their expert witness, Moses Schanfield, would testify that the state's results were inaccurate.

The state's first witness was none other than Ashley Stevens, who prosecutors continually – perhaps irritatingly – referred to as "little Ashley." On the stand, she testified to the same series of events she had told the police the previous September.

Under cross-examination, the defense tried to poke holes in her story. But Ashley stuck to her guns and stayed calm.

Charles Dorsey, with the state crime lab, had examined the biological evidence taken from Ashley's clothing and body.

He testified to his findings, first of which was the absence of sperm in the seminal fluid. This pointed to someone who had likely had a vasectomy.

In those days, DNA testing was still more than a decade away. But there were other tests that, while not as pinpoint accurate, could still exclude potential suspects. The tests that were available at the time could determine both the donor's blood type, as well as if they "secrete" a particular enzyme in their bodily fluids. These serological tests determined that the donor had type A blood, which is found in around 40 percent of the population, and that he was a "secretor," which accounts for only 28 percent of people.

Wayne matched all of these characteristics. According to Dorsey, the number of people who have had a vasectomy, have type A blood, and are a secretor is only 0.6 percent of the population – or about 60 in 10,000 people. Not exactly a slam-dunk, but the chance that Ashley had picked out some innocent rando who just so happened to have all three of these specific characteristics strained belief.

To counter that evidence, Wayne's defense wanted to bring in their own expert witness, Moses Schanfield, who had performed his own tests on the biological samples and determined that they did not, in fact, match Wayne.

But on the day Schanfield was supposed to testify, he was in the hospital – he had been stung by a bee and was deathly allergic. The defense asked to delay the trial, but Judge Yates denied it.

This was the hook that Wayne's defenders would go on to use to justify their belief that he was innocent. They would (and still do) claim that the DNA evidence exonerated him, but the corrupt judge refused to let Schanfield testify.

The truth is that Schanfield's allotype testing was inaccurate. Schanfield, who was a genetic expert out of Atlanta, claimed that the biological evidence could not have come from

Wayne. As Schanfield would later tell tabloid columnist Steve Dunleavy, "No way, zip, nada. Didn't happen. No way Dumond was the donor of that sperm ... The girl's scenario of the so-called crime couldn't have happened. I didn't believe anything she said."[1]

But Schanfield had made a very basic mistake (besides the fact that Wayne's seminal fluid contained no sperm): he had failed to account for a second genetic donor – Ashley. As in nearly every sexual assault, the victim's fluids had mixed with the attacker's, but Schanfield hadn't separated the two genetic profiles, making his test results worthless.

Back in the courtroom, the defense's other witnesses – Dusty, Jinger, and Wayne's brother Bobby – testified that Wayne had been sick, so he couldn't have committed the crime.

They all said, under oath, that Wayne had first seemed sick when he was attending his brother's birthday party the day before the attack, on September 10. Bobby testified that Wayne had left the party early – after an hour and a half. Dusty testified that that night, after they were home, she'd taken his temperature, and it had been 102.

Dusty and Jinger both testified that on the morning of September 11, Wayne had still been sick, but had gone in to work anyway.

They all testified that Wayne hadn't actually said anything to them about being sick, and they all used the same phrase to explain it away: "he never complains." When the prosecution grilled them on whether they had discussed their testimony, they swore they did not. But it surely must have stood out to the jury that his whole family was swearing by the same story in order to give him a supposed alibi when he didn't actually have one.

Jinger testified that when she got home from school at about ten minutes to four that afternoon, Wayne had been lying on the couch, "sick." She said she knew he was sick because she'd felt his forehead, and it had been hot.

Considering the timeframe of when the attack occurred, that would have given him about twenty minutes after dropping Ashley off at her home to drive back to his home – which, despite the defense's assertion, was entirely within the realm of possibility.

Wayne took the stand in his own defense, sprinkling in plenty of five-dollar words in his quiet, mumbling voice – Guy Reel describes his speaking style as "like an old Southern gentleman, but a redneck."[2] Under oath, he swore he came home from work early that day because he felt nauseated. He said he'd spent the afternoon watching TV, going back and forth between lying on the couch and lying in his bed.

He also swore he had never seen Ashley Stevens before, other than, as he testified, "I seen her picture in the paper a time or two." This was highly unlikely, as the news media don't, as a rule, identify minors who are victims of a crime, let alone run their photos.

Under cross examination, he explained that the reason he hadn't gone to a doctor was because it cost money – which is true enough. He also tried to claim that his eyes weren't, in fact, "crystal blue," as Ashley had described her attacker's. He said his eyes were green.

He finished his direct questioning by asserting, "With God as my witness, I didn't rape that girl."

The jury deliberated for three hours before finding Wayne guilty. He was later sentenced to life plus twenty years. While that might seem like an especially harsh sentence, as Sheriff Conlee would put it, "When you rape a cheerleader in a small town in Arkansas, this is what you get."

His attorneys immediately filed an appeal. But Wayne couldn't make his $300,000 appellate bond, so he was remanded to the custody of the State of Arkansas' Department of Corrections. He was driven to the Cummins unit by none other than Sheriff Conlee. Whatever conceit Conlee might have had while he was driving Wayne to what he believed would be a lifetime behind bars, it wouldn't last long.

The following fall, in 1986, African Americans in St. Francis County turned out in force for the election. For the first time ever, Coolidge Conlee was defeated at the polls – and that meant, for the first time in decades, he no longer had the power to shield himself from the law.

Two years after Conlee was voted out of office, things really started to unravel for him. In August of 1988, in a sweltering Forrest City courtroom without air conditioning, Wayne sued Conlee for violating his civil rights – specifically, a "tort of outrage" – by displaying his testicles.

Wayne was the first on the stand to testify, telling his story in his deep southern Arkansas accent. He described the attack just as he had to Lt. Ostermann: two men walked into his home, wearing stocking masks and rubber gloves, held him at gunpoint and forced him to the floor. They hogtied him, he said, then cut his testicles out and left him for dead. He repeated that one of them had said, "Mr. C would be proud."

He explained his reaction to Conlee's displaying his testicles: "And here this man is going to be atrocious enough to show severed body parts to people around town. I mean, it's bad enough that I had to be accused of a crime that I didn't commit, but to have the man to humiliate me that way by showing these parts – these private body parts..."[3]

He expressed his outrage that his testicles were flushed down the toilet: "They were mine. Those were my testicles.

He didn't have no right to take them, and he didn't have no right to show them around, and he didn't have no right to flush them down the toilet."[4] The injustice of it all, he testified, made him suicidal.

Next, Dusty took the stand and described her horror and rage at the attack, saying that "we felt that maybe the sheriff would put my breast in a jar. We didn't know what he would plan next..."[5]

Wayne's older son, Michael, testified as to what he saw when he came home from school that day, which no doubt must have touched the jurors.

It was through the testimony of other witnesses – and Conlee himself – that the more damning details about Wayne's castration came to light. Conlee testified that he had indeed scooped up the testicles in a matchbox, then got a jar and formaldehyde from Stevens' funeral home, with Stevens there. Later that evening, he testified, he took Stevens back to the steak dinner he'd been attending.

Conlee claimed that Ostermann had told him to take the testicles and preserve them as evidence, but then never came and picked them up, so he, Conlee, had just been holding on to them. Ostermann couldn't corroborate or dispute Conlee's testimony, since he had died in a plane crash the previous year.

Some of Stevens' employees testified that they had witnessed Stevens' wife come pull him out of that dinner party, stating someone from the sheriff's office needed him. They said they had seen Conlee at the funeral home with the testicles, and that Conlee had driven Stevens back to the dinner party, where Stevens talked about the castration – which had not been publicly reported yet.

It only took the jury an hour to come back with a guilty verdict, and in the end, they ordered Conlee to pay Wayne $150,000, which he used to pay his defense attorneys.

During the same month he lost the civil trial to Wayne, Conlee was back in the courtroom, facing another civil trial. This time, several former prisoners of his were suing him for the abuse he and his deputies had inflicted on them while they were in custody. The former prisoners won, and Conlee was ordered to pay out $1.5 million.

Just on the heels of that defeat, Conlee would face his final reckoning: the grand jury convened on the recommendation of Governor Clinton indicted him on 27 criminal counts, including racketeering, extortion, arson, and mail fraud.

His deputies Sambo Hughes and Danny Burns were also charged as his co-conspirators. While Burns was only facing drug charges for marijuana, Hughes was charged as an accomplice on most of the other charges and was facing up to 120 years in prison. So they both took plea deals in exchange for their testimony against Conlee. Burns' charge was downgraded to misdemeanor marijuana possession, and Hughes' were downgraded so that he would "only" face up to twenty years in prison and $250,000 in fines.

Thanks to some legal wrangling, several of Conlee's charges were dropped or combined with others, so that by the winter of 1988, he was facing eight counts of bribery, extortion, illegal gambling, and racketeering.

Conlee stood trial in the same courtroom, with the same judge, as he had in Wayne's civil trial against him.

Thanks to Hughes' testimony, as well as that of other county employees and people who had been extorted by Conlee, jurors saw plainly the pattern of criminality that Conlee had engaged in over the years. Just between 1983 and '84 alone, he had raked in almost $270,000 in bribes and extortion money.

But Conlee had enjoyed immunity for too long to think the law really applied to him. Even while the jury was out deliberating his verdict, Conlee stood in the hallway outside the courtroom smoking Kools and regaling reporters with tall tales of his days as a pit boss in Hot Springs, including a close call where he had left a club only minutes before a bomb went off. "That's when the mob was trying to take over," he reportedly said.[6]

The jury took just under four hours to reach a verdict. He was convicted on all counts.

After his conviction, he was sentenced to twenty years in prison, but he would end up only serving about two of them. In late April of 1990, the lifelong chain-smoker died of cardiac failure while undergoing open-heart surgery. His obituary, according to Guy Reel, "has to be one of the few in history that contains the word 'testicles.'"[7]

ENDNOTES:

1. Steve Dunleavy, "Clinton's Biggest Crime: Left Innocent Man in Jail for 14 Years," *New York Post*, September 21, 1999.

2. Guy Reel, personal interview with the author, February 14, 2024.

3. Guy Reel, *Unequal Justice: Wayne Dumond, Bill Clinton, and the Politics of Rape in Arkansas,* (Buffalo, New York: Prometheus Books, 1993), p. 201.

4. Reel, *Unequal Justice*, p. 202.

5. Reel, *Unequal Justice*, p. 203.

6. Dennis Byrd, "Conlee's trial holds ironic moment," *Arkansas Democrat*, November 8, 1988, p. 23.

7. Reel, *Unequal Justice*, p. 259.

Chapter 5: Bill and Hillary

The same year Conlee was convicted in federal court – 1988 – Bill Clinton was in the midst of his fourth term as governor – and his political star was rapidly rising. That year, he was serving as the chair of the National Governors' Association, and he was given a prominent timeslot to speak at the national Democratic National Convention.

While one of the more common insults thrown at Bill Clinton is "out-of-touch elite," nothing could be further from the truth. Born William Jefferson Blythe III in Hope, Arkansas (a most fortuitous name for a politician's hometown, as Mike Huckabee would later use to his advantage), he was the son of a widowed single mother. He was raised mostly by his grandmother until he was four, when his mother married Roger Clinton, an abusive alcoholic, and moved the family to Hot Springs (coincidentally, around the same time that Coolidge Conlee was running his illegal gambling houses there). As a young teenager, Bill once had to step in to protect his mother from Roger's abuse, though later, he did end up taking the Clinton last name.

Not long after that violent confrontation, he was selected to be a delegate to Boys' Nation, an American Legion civics-engagement program for high-school boys, in Washington, D.C. While there, he met and shook hands with then-President John F. Kennedy. He said that moment had a profound impact on him, setting him on the first steps of his political career.[1]

After high school, he went on to college, first earning a degree in international affairs from Georgetown University in 1968. He was named a Rhodes Scholar and went on to study in Oxford, England.

This being the late 1960s, the Vietnam War was still raging. Through his Rhodes Scholarship, Clinton was able to get an educational deferment to avoid the draft – something a lot of "fortunate sons" of the wealthy and powerful did as well. But somehow, they rarely faced the same criticism for it. Maybe it was because, while most powerful elites publicly supported the war – while quietly protecting themselves and their sons from serving in it (see Dick Cheney, George W. Bush, Mitch McConnell, Donald Trump, et al.) – Clinton was a working-class son who publicly spoke out against it.

It's now a common American myth that in the 1960s, everyone was a hippie, protesting against the war and for Civil Rights, burning bras and flags, smoking weed and dropping acid. But that wasn't the case. It's true that at the time, a lot of young people – and some older folks – were part of the overlapping subcultures commonly just called "youth culture," which included various left-wing activist groups. Thanks to these activists, women, Black folks, the LGBTQ+ community, and other marginalized groups achieved a great deal of social advancement.

But, as with any social change, there was the inevitable backlash, and the 1960s and '70s were more divided – and divisive – than at any time since the Civil War. Conservative politicians, preachers, pundits, and regular people frequently called anti-war protesters dirty Communists, traitors, and worse.

Richard Nixon won the presidential election of 1968 running on a "law and order" platform (a dog-whistle to Southern racists), and even as the Watergate scandal was breaking all around him, he was re-elected in 1972. Throughout his administration, Nixon used the power of the White House to target and eliminate the left. His FBI continued J. Edgar Hoover's COINTELPRO activities to illegally infiltrate, entrap, and prosecute leftist leaders and organizations under the guise of "national security." And he launched the War on Drugs specifically as a justification to lock up anti-war and Civil Rights activists.

The backlash didn't stop at the White House. Law enforcement agencies from the state police on down to local cops gleefully targeted "long-hairs" with overzealous enforcement for crimes both real and imagined. Peaceful protests were commonly met with violent police suppression, the most horrific of which being the Kent State Massacre in 1970, where Ohio National Guard troops opened fire on anti-war protestors, killing four and wounding nine.

In fact, it was this kind of police violence against protesters that changed a young Hillary Rodham's life. Raised as a Republican, her faith had been shaken by the assassinations of JFK and Martin Luther King, Jr. In 1968, she had just finished an internship working with House Republican leaders in D.C. and just happened to be in Chicago during the Democratic National Convention.

Hearing that Mayor Richard Daley was calling up 10,000 police and more than 5,000 National Guard troops in response to the anticipated protests, she "was filled with the sense that something momentous was in the offing."[2] So she and a friend decided to go see what was going down.

They walked into a war zone. Police in full riot gear were beating protesters and bystanders alike, herding them into streets filled with tear gas. Hillary and her friend fled in terror. From that experience, she renounced her Republican Party membership and became a Democrat.[3]

Hillary and Bill met while they were both in Yale Law School in 1971. After Hillary noticed that Bill wouldn't stop staring at her, she walked over and introduced herself. This would turn out to be the beginning of one of the most powerful, and consequential, partnerships in U.S. history.

The following year, the two worked on Democratic presidential candidate George McGovern's campaign. After his loss to Nixon, their paths briefly diverged. Hillary went to work for the Children's Defense Fund in Massachusetts, and Bill went back to his home state to teach law at the University of Arkansas.

In the spring of 1974, Hillary worked on the staff advising the House Judiciary Committee during the Watergate Investigation. As part of her duties, she listened to some of the infamous White House tapes.

After Nixon resigned in August of 1974, she joined Bill on the faculty at the U of A Law School. Though she was only there briefly, she founded the school's Legal Aid Clinic, which gives law students real-world experience while also providing poor Arkansans with free legal help.

In 1974, Bill took the first step on his own political career and ran for the U.S. House of Representatives. He lost to the popular Republican incumbent, John Paul Hammerschmidt, by less than two points.

After his loss, in 1975, the two were married in a small ceremony in the living room of the house Bill had purchased as a proposal gift. In what is still considered a controversial move fifty years later, she didn't take Bill's last name.

The following year, she went to Indiana to work on Jimmy Carter's presidential campaign, while Bill ran for – and won – state attorney general.

Then he set his sights higher. In 1979, Bill ran for governor of Arkansas and won. When he took office, he was only 32 years old, the youngest governor in the country at the time and the second youngest in Arkansas history. This earned him the nickname "the boy governor." Political cartoonists – especially George Fischer, Arkansas' most influential political cartoonist – often depicted him as a toddler in a sailor suit.

When, in her first public appearance as first lady of Arkansas, Hillary appeared on Jack Hill's program, *In Touch*, the cartoons and nicknames for her were not nearly as genteel.

At the time of the interview, she was in her early 30s – the same age as Bill – quite young for a first lady. And she was pretty far ahead of the curve in other ways, too.

For one, she didn't wear make-up – which was unheard of in political circles even in 1979 – but added to the fact that she hadn't taken her husband's last name, it apparently shook the veteran news anchor to the point of incredulity.

He started the interview off well enough, by introducing her with her impressive resume: "She was raised in the Chicago area; she has an undergraduate degree from Wellesley University, had a law degree from Yale University, and that's where she met her husband. Ms. Rodham is a former law professor at the University of Arkansas in Fayetteville and is a practicing attorney in Little Rock..."[4]

While I'm sure he had to keep it short for the intro, he left out a lot of her already impressive resume. The chyron identified her only as "Hillary Rodham – Governor's Wife."

Jack begins his interview with a fairly obvious question: "As the first lady for Arkansas now for about a month, do you feel comfortable in this new position, if it can be called a position?"

Hillary calmly responds with, "Well I think it is a position..." before detailing the difficulty of adjusting to the lack of privacy, as well as the political issues and hectic scheduling.

Jack's next few questions are what you would expect for a governor's wife – such as how they manage the issue of "living in a fishbowl" and not having enough time together. Hillary's answers are calm, affable – if rather long-winded.

But in a follow-up to his question about how they find time to be together, he starts to betray his own biases. He asks, "There are those in the audience who say, 'But aha, Ms. Rodham, if you just wouldn't be a practicing attorney, then, you see, that would eliminate some of the problem of not being together.'"

Hillary laughs it off, then explains, "I think people who are married to politicians are under a tremendous strain. Unless you have a pretty strong sense of your own self-identity, it becomes very easy to be buffeted by all the people that are around your husband." She then goes on to say that practicing law, besides being something she enjoys, "keeps me busy while he's gone." She never mentions the fact that she was the first woman to be made partner at the prestigious Rose Law Firm, the oldest law firm west of the Mississippi.

Jack again comes back to how non-traditional she is, stating that she doesn't seem to be interested in "state dinners, teas, and garden parties, the kinds of things we tend to associate with governor's wives."

Again, Hillary performs a masterful bit of rhetorical jiu-jitsu: "Well, that's not true; I'm interested in everything…social events and civic events, as well as my own professional life." She then apparently defends these various events as places where she can "learn new things and meet new people."

He asks her if she ever gets tired of people questioning why she kept her last name. She points out that since she was "older" (twenty-eight) when she married Bill, she already had an established law practice and had published under her own name. Plus, as she explains, she wanted to avoid the appearance of trading in on Bill's name, as well as keeping her professional life separate from his political life.

His follow-up is to ask if she thinks that keeping her last name might have painted her as "too progressive" and might have cost Bill some votes.

She responds with the fact that Anita Bryant – certainly no progressive – kept her own name. And as for losing any votes, she points out, rightfully, that people might vote against a politician for any variety of reasons. Left unspoken is the fact that Bill had won the election in a landslide.

Then Jack asks the question that encapsulates the essence of the entire interview: "You really don't fit the image we've created for the governor's wife in Arkansas. You're not a native; you've been educated in liberal eastern universities. You're less than forty; you don't have any children. You don't use your husband's last name; you practice law. Does it concern you that maybe other people feel that you don't fit the image that we have created for the governor's wife in Arkansas?"

She doesn't hesitate or falter. "No, because, just as I said before, I think that each person should be assessed and judged on that person's own merits. ... That doesn't bother me."

Despite how it might have looked to viewers, Jack said Hillary "simply dazzled" him. After the interview, he would tell Anne that he was shocked by Hillary's glasses and lack of make-up. "But then," he reportedly told Anne, "she opened her mouth, and I totally forgot the way she looked, I was so taken aback by her intelligence and her ability to articulate." According to Anne, he was "blown away" and "spent the rest of his life convinced Rodham was the alpha brain of the Clinton team."[5]

Yet many of Jack's viewers came away with the opposite impression. It was mostly from this interview that the stereotype of Hillary as a man-hating feminist (and possible closeted lesbian) first began to emerge in Arkansas.

The following year, 1980, was a turning point in many ways. It was the year that the Satanic Panic began to take hold of America's imagination, mostly thanks to the publication of *Michelle Remembers*, a lurid (and later debunked) account of one woman's childhood of abuse by a Satanic cult. Soon people were seeing Satanists in daycares, rock music, fantasy role-playing games, and even children's toys.

In that presidential election, thanks to the efforts of Jerry Falwell Sr.'s "Moral Majority" (which, to quote a popular slogan at the time, was neither), twice-divorced Hollywood actor Ronald Reagan sealed the white Evangelical vote against the Navy veteran and Sunday School teacher Jimmy Carter. This moment is widely regarded as a watershed moment in American politics: the wedding of the Republican Party with conservative Christianity.

Not coincidentally, it was also when the right began ramping up its attacks against the left in general and Democrats in particular. From church pulpits to AM radio studios, from poorly mimeographed newsletters to slick fundraising mailers, allegations and accusations against the left continued where the John Birch Society left off. They spread hysterical conspiracy theories about "Godless" Democrats, leftists, and feminists, designed to terrify voters.[6] And one of the most common accusations against the left and Democrats was "baby killers."

Ever since the 1976 Republican presidential primary, when Jesse Helms and his allies pushed an anti-abortion plank into the party's platform, the hatred and fearmongering about abortion began pouring out of AM talk radio shows, pulpits, and religious media of every type. This medical procedure, which, before that, had only been an issue for Catholics, was repeatedly described as "murdering babies" and even likened to the Holocaust. This rhetoric proved to be extremely useful in riling up the base – some, to the point of committing violence.

Starting in 1978, when a clinic in Oregon was set ablaze, attacks against abortion clinics (and the people who work in them) began to intensify. By 1983, there had been twenty-nine bombings and arsons of abortion clinics around the country. In 1984 alone, there were twenty-five bombings and arsons.[7]

By the mid-'80s, nearly every clinic in the United States had, at one point or another, been subjected to "intimidating, coercive, or violent tactics." And the larger anti-abortion movement tacitly condoned the violence. In 1985, at a "pro-life" convention in Chicago, organizers handed out pins that included an image of explosives, and the sign over the doors read, "WELCOME CONVENTIONEERS, HAVE A BLAST!"[8]

Nearly all of the attackers considered themselves Christians, and many were Christian nationalists, advocating for the destruction of secular government and the imposition of "biblical" law.

Not coincidentally, beginning around that same time, a wave of violent "militia" groups began popping up all over the country, starting with the white supremacist anti-government group, Posse Comitatus. While not all militias were based on white supremacy, sovereign citizen anti-governmentalism, or Christian nationalism, a Venn diagram of the three would look like a circle.

Motivated by a lack of faith in (or outright hostility to) the government and institutions of civil society, they stockpiled food, supplies, and weapons. They also engaged in paramilitary training exercises on rural compounds in preparation for the total socio-economic breakdown they believed was imminent – the moment when "the shit hits the fan," or SHTF, as they put it.

Starting in the 1980s, several of these groups, like Posse Comitatus and The Order, began engaging in acts of terrorism – though nowhere near as prolifically as the anti-abortion terrorists. Their actions ranged from threats to bombings (mostly unsuccessful) to assassinations – the most well-known of which was the murder of Jewish talk radio host Alan Berg in 1983.

***

Back in Arkansas, this unholy alliance had not quite taken hold, at least not on a large scale. The state was still solidly Democratic, at least on the down-ballot races.

Despite the accusations thrown his way, Bill was no hippie – he had built his brand as a centrist problem-solver who often reached across the aisle – but he had been an outspoken opponent of the Vietnam War and would later admit to "trying" marijuana in college, but "didn't inhale." Importantly, one hallmark of his political career was his promotion of Civil Rights, earning him the support of Arkansas' substantial African American community. And in the Bible Belt, at least among the reactionaries, racists, and religious types, Bill and Hillary represented everything they hated: anti-American Communists, pot smokers, race traitors, and radical feminists.

When Bill came up for re-election that year, he went up against former Democrat and recent Republican convert Frank White. And even though Bill had only been in office for two years, he'd already made plenty of Arkansans mad at him. There had been reporting of mishandling of funds at various state agencies. Then there was his tax hike on car registrations, which was predictably unpopular. His biggest issue was far worse – and it wasn't even his doing. In early May of 1980, then-President Jimmy Carter sent about 120,000 Cuban refugees to Fort Chaffee, near the city of Fort Smith, as a stopover before being transferred elsewhere.[9]

Clinton publicly supported Carter's decision, but he apparently underestimated the depth of anti-immigrant prejudice in the state. And even worse, Carter hadn't given the state any resources to handle this massive influx of people.[10]

So on May 26, 1980, one day before the primaries, around three hundred refugees who had been housed at the base turned over the barricades and escaped, fleeing into the surrounding county.[11] Since the refugees weren't prisoners, federal troops were not authorized to use violence to force them to remain in the fort. Bowing to popular outrage, Clinton ordered Arkansas National Guard troops to assist local and state police to prevent the refugees from leaving again.

The refugees were understandably upset at being treated as prisoners, and alleged that federal troops would beat them. The refugees staged hunger strikes in protest. Meanwhile, the citizens of Barling, a small town close to the base, were arming themselves in preparation for an immigrant "invasion." Tensions were extremely high. Then, on the night of June 1, 1980, the refugees at Fort Chaffee rioted. The press called it "a war zone." Buildings were set on fire. Thousands of angry refugees charged the gate, unhindered by federal troops. About 200 refugees escaped and ran down Highway 22 towards Barling. At the end of the night, five refugees had been shot, and sixty-two other people were injured.[12]

Despite the fact that Clinton had no control over this disaster – and in fact had used what little power he did have to try and contain it – his public support of taking in the refugees led many Arkansans to feel like he bore some responsibility for it.

Frank White used the Cuban Refugee Crisis to great advantage in his first election campaign, along with the unpopularity of the car registration tax hike. Otherwise, he ran a fairly tame race. There were no allegations of extramarital affairs, criminal activities, or other debauchery (at least in the press). The fact that White was a devout Baptist who supported teaching Christian "creation science" in public schools likely solidified Evangelical support behind him. To the surprise of nearly everyone, White won the election. His defeat of Clinton – an incumbent Democrat – was considered a stunning upset in a state still stanchly loyal to Democrats (at least at the state and local level). In fact, White was so taken off guard, he came into office without a clear legislative agenda.

Bill would say that this loss had been one of the most painful experiences in his life. Hillary would later say that after this, he became much more cautious and moderate.

Bill returned to the campaign trail in 1982 with a TV commercial acknowledging that he'd made mistakes, but had learned from them and was committed to listening to voters' concerns. His new slogan was, "You can't lead without listening."

And while White criticized Clinton as an out-of-touch liberal elite, Clinton fired back that White was in bed with the big utility companies, and was responsible for letting them raise rates on consumers – as well as raising drug prices for Medicaid recipients – while giving big corporations millions in tax breaks. It worked. Bill Clinton won back the Governor's Mansion with almost fifty-five percent of the vote. Young, good-looking, and charismatic, he would go on to be elected governor five more times, making him only one month shy of being the longest-serving governor of the state, behind Orval Faubus.

During his time in office, he focused on bringing industry and investments into Arkansas, which was still pretty much a backwater state whose biggest industry was agriculture. His other legislative focus was education, taking on the powerful state teachers' union to push for basic skills testing for teachers to ensure that every Arkansan would get a good quality education.

On the other hand, that much time in office offers a lot of opportunities for a lot of scandals, even for the most straight-laced of politicians (if such a creature exists). And Bill Clinton – a moderate, middle-of-road centrist – was nowhere near "straight-laced," at least by the standards of the South's archconservatives in the 1970s and '80s.

While he was nowhere near the radical degenerate the right painted him as, it was pretty much an open secret that Bill had a wandering eye. But during his time in the Governor's Mansion, the press still operated under the old "gentlemen's agreement" that a politician's personal life was just that – personal. By the time Clinton declared his candidacy for president in 1992, that gentlemen's agreement would be torn to shreds.

ENDNOTES:

1. Clinton House Museum, "William Jefferson Clinton."

2. Michael D'Antonio, *The Hunting of Hillary*, (New York, New York: Thomas Dunne Books, 2020), p. 21.

3. D'Antonio, *The Hunting of Hillary*, p. 21.

4. Hillary Rodham, interview by Jack Hill, *In Focus*. KAIT, January 1979.

5. Dale Carpenter and Robert Cochran, *Reporting for Arkansas: The Documentary Films of Jack Hill*, (Fayetteville, Arkansas, University of Arkansas Press, 2022), p. 59.

6. Gene Lyons, "The roots of the Clinton smear," Salon. com, February 5, 1998.

7. Clarkson, Frederick, "Anti-Abortion Movement Marches On After Two Decades of Arson, Bombs and Murder," *The Intelligence Report*, September 15, 1998.

8. Miller, Cassie, "The Violent History of the Anti-Abortion Movement," *The Intelligence Report*, June 13, 2024.

9. Clinton House Museum, "1980."

10. Clinton House Museum, "1980."

11. Clinton House Museum, "1980."

12. Clinton House Museum, "1980."

Chapter 6: The Early Push to Free Wayne Dumond

Cummins Prison, home to the state's execution chamber, sits about an hour's drive southeast of Little Rock, near Pine Bluff, surrounded by fields of soybeans, canola, and other crops. Originally built to house Black inmates, it began to be integrated in the 1930s, and now prisoners of all races work in the broiling sun, tending those crops.

For decades, Cummins had been plagued by corruption, violence, and unfit living conditions. It's probably most well known for being the inspiration for the movie *Brubaker*, which was based on a book written by former Cummins prison warden Thomas Murton. Arkansas native son Johnny Cash, along with June Carter Cash and other big-name artists, performed a concert there in 1969 to shine a light on the need for prison reform.[1]

Through years of advocacy like theirs, by the time Wayne was sent there in 1986, it had finally come into compliance with federal law, but was still one of the hardest prisons in America.[2]

He spent fifteen days in the diagnostic unit before being transferred to the main Cummins Unit. His first year or so there, Wayne was, as he put it, a "troublemaker," starting fights with guards and other inmates, and at one point, attempting suicide. He said he got nine disciplinary charges – all "phony" or set-ups, according to him – and six of them sent him into solitary confinement for thirty days each.[3]

Back on the outside, Dusty had moved up to Fayetteville to live with the fundamentalist preacher Jay Cole and his family.

Cole was born in Paragould, a tiny town in northeast Arkansas, in 1929. He attended Hardin-Simmons, a private Baptist university in Abilene, Texas, where he met his wife-to-be, Thelma.

He served in the Air Force during the Korean Conflict, then attended Drury College and then Oklahoma Baptist University as a ministerial student. While still in school there, he served as pastor for the First Baptist Church in Rosedale, Oklahoma.

Pastoring wasn't his only skill, though; he was also a mechanical engineer. He worked at a few insurance companies in that capacity before striking out and establishing several electronics businesses. Most of those businesses catered to Christian churches and missionary groups, in one way or another.

Cole, Thelma, and their three children, had moved to the Fayetteville area in 1976, to a ranch-style brick house set far back from a dirt road in rural Washington County, west of the city limits. There he founded Mission Fellowship Bible Church, a fundamentalist Baptist church, in his home.

He also started a business, Mission Service Supply, which sold blank tapes and high-speed tape duplication equipment to churches, missionary groups, and other religious organizations. This business – which he'd run some version of for years – put him in contact with a lot of other clergy, especially Evangelicals, since in those pre-social-media days, the way to get your message out was to create and mass-duplicate cassettes or VHS tapes and then distribute them to churches and other organizations.

But most of his time was devoted to his third passion: his crusade to put his God "back" into American government. He first founded Save Our Nation, a political action committee "to help defend our United States of America from it's [sic] most dreaded enemy, Secular Humanism" and to recruit, train, and promote Christians into leadership positions in government.[4] It was also the name of his AM radio talk show, where he and his occasional co-host, Johnny Tittle, railed against secular humanism, feminism, homosexuality, and the "God-hating" ACLU.

Later, in the early 1990s, he was a founding member of, and served as chaplain for, the Washington County Militia, whose mission was to not only protect their "God given" Second Amendment rights, but also to "fight tyranny through the use of arms." Such tyranny, according to their website, includes "socialist enemies" in the government who promote a "Luciferian New World Order."[5] Even if you didn't attend his church or listen to the show, most anyone who lived in Northwest Arkansas in the late 1980s or early '90s knew who Jay Cole was.

If your TV could get local station 40/29 (which wasn't always the case, since the steep valleys often lost TV signals in those pre-digital days), your Saturday morning cartoons often came with a bizarre serving of fire and brimstone. In between Scooby Doo and Bugs Bunny, viewers got the usual ads for sugary cereal and toys, but they also would also have the unsettling experience of Rev. Jay Cole's commercials.

Since this was in the internet's embryonic days, no recordings of these commercials exist. I'll have to describe them from memory, which I have confirmed with other locals who remember seeing them (and everyone who saw them, remembers them):

The camera opens on a stark scene, evoking a hostage video. Seemingly lit only by an overhead fluorescent light, a thin, elderly white man sits, center frame, behind a blank desk.

The entire background is filled with an imposing American flag.

The man is dressed in an ill-fitting suit and wears square, wire-framed bifocals so thick they obscure his eyes, even though he's staring directly at the camera. Bushy eyebrows protrude above them like insect antennae; his thin lips have a distinctive blue cast to them. Though his hairline is receding, his grey hair is still thick and wavy, combed up in an Elvis-style pompadour.

When he begins speaking, his soft Southern drawl sounds like a pa-paw who's not angry, just disappointed. The script of one of his commercials is still on his website:

"One of the most frequently heard statements is 'You can't legislate morality.' Isn't that strange? I read quite a list of morality issues legislated by both state and federal law, and all of them are taken from the Bible. There's murder, adultery, homosexuality, robbery, lying, and a host of others.

"But suppose the Supreme Court decides to change the word 'murder' to 'population control' for all over age fifty, as they did the word 'abortion' for unborn babies under nine months of age. What would we say then about legislating morality?"

His voice gets a little more forceful as the monologue continues: "The truth is, recreational sex, personal convenience, and downright greed outweigh human decency and respect, a rapidly disappearing quality. The once treasured WORD of GOD is now neglected or ignored by many who call themselves Christian, and is rejected by others. Sanity tells us to consider history. EVERY nation that has gone the way America is going has been destroyed."

Then, he pleads, sadly, "America, wake up before it's too late."[6]

He ends the diatribe as he does all of them, with a line that is still, decades later, burned into the brains of many Fayettevillians: "I'm Jay Cole."

And then you'd be back to watching Bugs Bunny re-runs.

But it wasn't just the weirdly terrifying commercials or his rabidly right-wing talk show that made Jay Cole into something of a local personality. Because he didn't just rant on his commercials and radio show; he frequently took his reactionary beliefs to the streets of Fayetteville.

Home to the University of Arkansas, Fayetteville, like most college towns, skews young and liberal, so Cole had plenty to get offended by. He would regularly show up to protest local Pride events and, in the words of one long-time resident, "act like an asshole." His antics led many to refer to him as the "proto-Fred Phelps."

He also regularly started beefs with the students at Fayetteville High School. In one, he got mad at the yearbook staff because they allowed a local store named Condom Sense to purchase an ad. The school didn't cow to his threats, though. Instead, they told him that if he didn't like it, he could purchase an ad for himself. So he did – a large spread "advertising" for abstinence.

Another beef he had with them was similar: he wanted the school newspaper to publish a whole insert on "The Dangers of Homosexuality." The pamphlet had some pretty graphic – and incorrect – descriptions of gay sex in it, including the phrase "fecal swallowing," so the staff rejected it.

Thanks to these kinds of antics, at least in Fayetteville, yanking his chain became something of a local pastime. One high school student made a T-shirt with the words "I AM THE ANTI-COLE" on it. Condom Sense adopted the unofficial slogan, "Proudly Pissing Off Jay Cole Since 1993." People would use "Jay Cole" as their usernames on bulletin board systems and other pseudonymous platforms, just so they could say his signature catchphrase, "I'm Jay Cole."

But outside of the Fayetteville area, he wasn't known by many. He seemed like just one more right-wing loony. Except he did have one very important friend: a fellow pastor named Mike Huckabee – but we'll get to that in a minute.

Dusty apparently impressed Cole (and everyone else) that she and Wayne were good Christians, with a "a notable history in the Baptist community, heading the youth department of a church in Forrest City."[7]

But maybe more than Dusty's lobbying, or Wayne's declarations of faith, what convinced Cole was his absolute *hatred* of the Clintons. At this point, the only allegation about Clinton's involvement in the case was that because Ashley was related to him, Conlee (also a Democrat, but of the more Dixiecrat persuasion) had railroaded Wayne.

But in Cole's worldview, it had to be something much more sinister. Bill and Hillary stood for everything that he – and most fundamentalist evangelicals – opposed: part of the "pro-abortion" Democratic party, feminist, and pro-Civil Rights (Cole was, in private at least, quite racist). And of course, since Wayne was a "good Christian," there was no way he could be guilty of such an awful crime.

Cole said he "conducted an investigation" into the case by questioning 100 people, mostly other Evangelicals, about Wayne's case. "I talked to [Dumond's] pastor and the high school principal of the school — not a single one of them said anything bad about him," Cole said.[8]

So Cole agreed to become Wayne's "spiritual director" in prison. He told a *Los Angeles Times* reporter, "...we'd sit and talk and pray for two hours, and other times he'd call me on the phone a lot. Collect. He was just wanting to know if I'd made any headway finding people who could help his situation," he said. "He was a nice fella, and it was hard to believe he could have done what he was accused of doing."[9]

Maybe thanks to Cole's influence, Wayne stopped getting in fights and, instead, got very religious.

Besides ministering to Wayne in prison, Cole joined Dusty in actively campaigning for his release, organizing letter-writing campaigns and talking about it on his radio show. While there aren't any records of the show in existence, tracking the spread of misinformation like a virus points to Cole's radio show as "patient zero" in expanding Clinton's supposed role in Wayne's case. It was around this time, and in this Evangelical/AM talk show media sphere, that Clinton went from simply the powerful man the victim was related to, into actively participating in railroading Wayne into prison or even personally arranging his castration – or both. Cole's rabidly right-wing audience had been primed by years of propaganda to believe the worst about Bill Clinton, so it wasn't a hard sell to them. Meanwhile, Dusty and Jay weren't the only ones working hard to get Wayne released.

Since Jack had been forced out of KAIT, the Hills had been going through some tough times. He'd been doing any kind of work he could get to pay the bills, but he itched to get back into journalism. Problem was, with Conlee's libel suit hanging over his head, no news outlets would touch him.

But there was one place that was amenable to hiring him: the *Arkansas Democrat*. Its managing editor, Bob Starr, who was often described as "flamboyant" and opinionated, was a staunch Clinton critic. So Jack approached him about continuing the investigation into Coolidge Conlee.[10] Starr agreed to bring Jack on the payroll to write the series – but only as a freelancer. Working with print reporter Jan Meins, the two ran a series of exposés titled "The St. Francis Machine," the first of which was printed in early April 1986.

The second article in the series was devoted to Wayne's case, pointing the finger at Conlee for the castration.

Like Cole, Starr was also putting his platform to good use, publishing regular editorials in support of Wayne. Most of these were based on the belief that Wayne had been framed by Conlee and his men, and that Clinton was turning a blind eye – or actively blocking Wayne from getting an appeal – because of his relation to the victim and/or the Democratic political machine in St. Francis. There was also a letter-writing campaign in the editorial pages of the *Democrat* and other southeast Arkansas newspapers. Judging from the talking points, it was likely to have been organized through Dusty, Cole, and the religious side of the movement. The vitriol towards Ashley in these letters is shocking by today's standards: one letter to the *Arkansas Democrat* in 1988 states, "I question whether that girl in Forrest City was even raped" and that a new trial would exonerate Wayne.[11]

While Jack was freelancing for the *Democrat*, Anne threw herself utterly into helping him investigate Wayne's case. She took down every rumor about Ashley, which were basically the same allegations made against any woman who accuses a man of sexual assault: mostly, that she had been having sex with her boyfriend and cried "rape" to cover it up.[12]

To Anne's credit, in her notes, she does go through all the rumors logically and concludes that Ashley had indeed been raped. She just can't bring herself to believe that Wayne was her rapist.[13]

Through her crusade, Anne made contact with Guy Reel, the reporter for the Memphis *Commercial Appeal* who had broken the story about Conlee displaying Wayne's testicles. He said he was in Little Rock, covering an unrelated case, when someone tapped him on the shoulder. That someone was Anne.[14]

Guy said that after that, he worked closely with Anne on the case,[15] but in their zeal to find any evidence to exonerate Wayne, they might have crossed some ethical lines. They allegedly sent money to "witnesses" who were behind bars, and were also alleged to have given one source an expense card. These sources would later claim in statements to the state police that Anne was "feeding" them information about the case.[16] It's important to note, in fairness, that one of the "witnesses" had previously admitted to lying in sworn affidavits.

By 1987, thanks to the Hills, Dusty, Jay Cole, and Bob Starr, there was much more public support for Wayne's cause. They had, as Max Brantley, former editor of the *Arkansas Times,* put it, wanted to make it "too neat," a story that Wayne was an innocent man who'd been done wrong by the power structure in Forrest City.[17] And he was only being kept in prison because Clinton was related to the victim (which many didn't even believe had been raped at all).

That year, during a press conference about a completely unrelated matter, out of left field, Clinton was questioned why he hadn't done anything about the corruption in St. Francis County. His response was that he wasn't aware of it.

So Jack aimed to remedy that. He wrote directly to Governor Clinton. In his letter, he said that many in St. Francis County had the impression that Clinton was tied to Conlee and his political machine. He also told Clinton that his (Clinton's) credibility was damaged because he'd pushed through Gene Raff, Conlee's political crony, to the State Police Commission.[18]

In response, Clinton ordered the state police, along with the FBI, to meet with Jack to look into Wayne's castration and "the possible involvement of public officials." But while Jack felt like the meeting went nowhere, a grand jury was later convened on Clinton's recommendation. That grand jury would go on to indict Conlee for the crimes that would send him to prison.

Jack had also sent a copy of his letter to Clinton to Charlie Thompson, a producer at *20/20*. Together with Guy Reel, they worked with Charlie on the script for the segment "The Law and Sheriff Conlee," which aired in January 1989, just a couple months after Conlee's conviction.

Soon after that episode aired, Wayne was interviewed in prison by the *Arkansas Democrat*. No doubt hoping that Conlee's conviction would bolster his chances for an appeal, Wayne again insisted that he was an innocent man. And he made sure to bring up what had been done to him while he was out on bail.

But this time, his story included a new detail: now, Wayne claimed that his attackers had forced him to perform oral sex on one of them. This was the first time he had made this allegation – he never mentioned it in his original police statement or on the stand at his civil trial against Conlee. But from this point on, it would become part of the canon, repeated in interviews, books, and articles across the nation.

Charlie Thompson's exposé helped Wayne much more than just getting his story out to a national audience. According to Guy, Charlie actively helped Wayne's cause by putting him in touch with Little Rock attorney John Hall, considered one of the best defense attorneys in the state, who agreed to represent Wayne pro bono. In addition, Hall hired Anne on part time as a research assistant for the case.[19]

But even with so many people on his side, Wayne's appeals were going nowhere. He requested new trials based on the claim that the state hadn't provided the defense with exonerating evidence – namely, the fact that his fingerprints weren't found on Ashley's car, which is neither exculpatory nor inculpatory. They tried to get a new trial based on the flawed serological tests done by Moses Schanfield.

All of his requests for appeals through the Arkansas Supreme Court were denied. So he tried his luck with the federal courts. He argued again that Schanfield's tests should be used in a new trial, and that his sentence was excessive. Those went nowhere as well.

After one magistrate judge turned down Wayne's appeal, Dusty took it upon herself to write to him: "You are part of a travesty of justice in Arkansas," she wrote. "You may wear a federal title but you are a friend and neighbor of Bill Clinton...you could do nothing else but cover up for him."[20]

She goes on excoriating him for two pages, using terms like "supposed victim" and "supposed rape." In one part, she says the St. Francis Political Machine "put him in a bag and threw him in prison for life. Well, you may not know it, and for sure you do not care, but God is in that bag with him and even with you putting another anchor on that bag to hold him there, Wayne Dumond will be coming out of that prison one day." She finishes, "What you sow, you will reap, God promises us that."[21] She sent copies of the letter to several Arkansas newspapers, as well.

Now with no more judicial recourse, his attorney took a different approach: he wrote to the state Board of Pardons and Paroles to ask for clemency.

So in June of 1990, the board met to vote on Wayne's petition. Maybe Wayne's new allegation that he'd been sexually assaulted as well as castrated had played on the board's sympathy. Maybe Conlee's recent conviction lent Wayne's story more credence. Maybe it was his adamant declarations of being "saved." Or maybe it was the result of the years of campaigning on his behalf. But on June 26, 1990, the parole board voted unanimously to recommend that Gov. Clinton grant Wayne's petition for clemency, meaning he would be released immediately.

However, the parole board's recommendation wasn't the final say – it needed Clinton's approval. When the parole board's recommendation crossed his desk the next day, he refused to sign it. When questioned, Clinton said he didn't want to free him when his case was still going through the appeals process. More likely, he didn't want to touch such a controversial case in an election year.

There was outrage on both sides of the issue. On Wayne's side, they felt this proved that Clinton was out to get Wayne. Others who knew the danger he posed came forward in support of keeping Wayne behind bars.

So, a month later, the parole board decided to hold another, full hearing on Wayne's case. The hearing was held in two parts. The first part was held in Forrest City. There, they spoke with Ashley and her family, as well as the Forrest City woman who had accused Wayne of raping her back in the 1970s. They all told the board they feared for their lives if he was released. They also presented the board with a petition signed by fifty-five people urging them not to release Wayne.[22]

The second part of the hearing was held at Cummins. There, Wayne said that the original Forrest City victim had been lying about him. He told them that at the time, he'd been selling drugs, and she'd offered to "take it out in trade," so to speak. "The next thing I know, she was yelling 'rape,'" he said.[23]

After hearing both sides, the parole board decided to "split the baby." They recommended that Wayne's sentence be commuted (i.e., reduced), though they couldn't agree on what his new sentence should be. So, while Wayne was still in prison, this was the first step towards his eventual freedom.

ENDNOTES:

1. Colin Woodward, "Cummins Unit," Encyclopedia of Arkansas, June 16, 2023.

2. Woodward, "Cummins Unit."

3. Guy Reel, *Unequal Justice: Wayne Dumond, Bill Clinton, and the Politics of Rape in Arkansas,* (Buffalo, New York: Prometheus Books, 1993). p. 165.

4. "Our Mission," Save Our Nation.

5. "Manual," Washington County Militia.

6. "Audio/Video Spots," Save Our Nation.

7. Max Blumenthal, "The Real Mike Huckabee," *The Nation*, January 28, 2008.

8. Blumenthal, "The Real Mike Huckabee."

9. Richard A. Serrano, "Parole officials: Huckabee pushed rapist's release," *Los Angeles Times*, December 8, 2007.

10. Reel, *Unequal Justice,* p. 141.

11. Joyce Mayberry, Letter to the Editor, publication unknown.

12. Special Collections, Anne Hill notebook, Jack Hill papers, Series 3, Box 43, folders 7-8.

13. Anne Hill notebook, folder 8.

14. Guy Reel, personal interview with the author, February 14, 2024.

15. Reel, personal interview.

16. Special Collections, Arkansas State Police interviews with Patricia Roberts DeVasier and Dale Sersey, Jack Hill papers, Series 3, Box 43, Folder 13.

17. Max Brantley, personal interview, January 2021.

18. Reel, *Unequal Justice,* pp. 176-177.

19. Reel, *Unequal Justice,* pp. 176-177.

20. Special Collections, Jack E. Hill papers, letter from Dusty Dumond to Judge David Young, February 13, 1989. Series 3, Box 43, Folder 2.

21. Special Collections, letter from Dusty Dumond.

22. Jan Meisel, "Fears Dumond, victim testifies," *Arkansas Democrat*, September 5, 1990.

23. Joe Farmer, "Parole board hears Dumond's side," *Arkansas Democrat*, September 13, 1990.

Chapter 7: Clinton's First Presidential Run

The fact that Clinton had decided to run for governor again in 1990 was a bit of a surprise for many, both in Arkansas and the wider country. Arkansas media had been questioning him about a possible presidential bid as early as 1987, when he'd traveled to Iowa, New Hampshire, and other states, clearly to survey his presidential prospects.[1] Then there was his positive debut at the 1988 Democratic National Convention. His political star was on the rise. He'd even called a press conference, where everyone expected he would announce his candidacy. But in a last-minute decision, he stated that he would not run for president that year, explaining that it would be too hard on Hillary and Chelsea (who was only eight at the time).[2]

That led most politicos – state and national – to assume that he was sure to run for president in 1992. The problem was, that would fall right in the middle of Arkansas' four-year gubernatorial term.

So, back on the Arkansas gubernatorial campaign trail, the big question for Clinton was, if he were to be re-elected governor, would he serve his whole term for Arkansas? Or would he jump ship to run for president?

In one televised debate, Clinton assured the people of Arkansas that if he were re-elected, he would commit to serving the full four years as their governor. It must have worked, because he was re-elected with more than fifty-seven percent of the vote.

But his presidential ambitions were still there. In 1991, he went on what he called a "secret tour," traveling around the state without notifying the press, to gauge public opinion about him breaking that pledge.[3]

Apparently, Arkansans didn't care too deeply one way or another. So, on October 3, 1991, on the steps of the Old State House Museum – the former capitol building – Bill Clinton announced he was running for president of the United States.

However, when Clinton had wowed the Democratic National Convention in 1988, his fellow Democrats weren't the only ones who saw presidential potential in the young governor. Lee Atwater, former chair of the Republican National Committee and adviser to Reagan and Bush (the first one), saw it too. And he intended to nip a potentially powerful political rival in the bud. He encouraged, and funded, former Democrat Tommy Robinson's gubernatorial campaign against Clinton. "We're going to take Tommy Robinson and use him to throw everything we can think of at Clinton – drugs, women, whatever works," Atwater reportedly said. He committed to providing top pollsters, consultants, media people, and, of course, money to the Robinson campaign.[4]

But apparently Republicans weren't the only ones who played dirty. According to Joe Conason and Gene Lyons, a few weeks before the May 1990 state primary, copies of Robinson's confidential medical records were leaked to the press. In those records, Robinson had admitted to drinking upwards of a pint of bourbon every day and taking sedatives known to cause paranoia.[5] In Arkansas at the time, the two largest religious denominations were Baptist and Church of Christ – both of which forbid drinking alcohol. So the Robinson allegations were a bombshell.[6]

Another stroke of bad luck hit the Robinson campaign in March of 1990 when Atwater, its main strategist and supporter, fell ill with a brain tumor (which would eventually kill him) .[7]

The final, fatal blow came on the day of the primaries. Well over 500,000 Democrats voted in the Republican primary[8] – which is legal under the state's open primary system – handing the Republican nomination to Sheffield Nelson.

While Nelson didn't have the support of the Washington Republican establishment behind him, he did have some unofficial help from powerful allies – as well as another former Democrat with a grudge against him.

In 1988, Clinton had hired Larry Nichols, a former advertising jingle writer, as a marketing consultant to the state's Development and Finance Authority. Nichols immediately started drawing attention to himself by bragging to anyone who would listen that he was actually a secret CIA operative. As laughable as this was, he wasn't entirely lying.

It turns out Nichols was working with the CIA ... illegally. An Associated Press investigation uncovered that he had been working with Oliver North and his associates to funnel money and other assistance to the Nicaraguan Contras, in direct violation of U.S. law.

Along with his business partner Darrell Glascock (a Republican political operative who had publicly challenged Clinton to take a drug test in 1986), he'd used his marketing expertise to produce pro-Contra propaganda videos while at his ADFA office. Even worse, he'd made nearly 650 long-distance calls – on his ADFA office phone – to Contra leaders and politicians who supported them (including Tommy Robinson). For those of you too young to remember "long distance," these calls were charged by the minute, and international calls – such as those to Central America – could be as high as $4 or more a minute.

When questioned, Nichols claimed the calls were for state bond sales – but it didn't take a lot of digging to disprove that.

Through this investigation, it was also uncovered that Nichols had previously faced multiple counts of theft by deception – i.e., fraud – in several Arkansas counties. But he had negotiated with the courts to avoid prosecution by promising to pay restitution to his victims. He then promptly declared bankruptcy and never paid up.[9]

Once all this came to light in September 1988, Clinton demanded Nichols' resignation. Nichols, seemingly unaware that Clinton had actually done him a solid by not having him criminally charged, never forgave Clinton.

So in 1990, Nichols (unofficially) went to work for Nelson Sheffield's campaign. In an October surprise, he filed a $3 million libel suit against Clinton, accusing him of wrongful termination. To kick it off, Nichols held a press conference to announce the filing on the steps of the Little Rock courthouse, where he handed out copies of his lawsuit to the reporters gathered there. These copies came with an important appendix: a list of five women who Nichols alleged that Clinton had slept with and used ADFA money to pay off. One of those women was Gennifer Flowers, an aspiring singer whom Nichols had worked with before though his marketing firm.

The reporters, thankfully, did their due diligence and followed up with the women. All five of them strenuously denied ever having slept with Clinton, let alone being paid off by him. Flowers, interestingly, threatened to sue for defamation if her name was published with these false accusations.

So, faced with the utter collapse of Nichols' allegations, Arkansas media outlets refused to publish the women's names. His lawsuit was later dismissed by the judge for lack of evidence.

That should have been the end of the whole affair, but the political and social world of 1990 was far different than what it had been just a decade earlier. First, while the Little Rock press corps was still playing by the old rules of journalistic integrity, the national media landscape had changed – for the worse.

For decades, the news media had held a sort of "gentleman's agreement" that the president's personal life was just that – personal. Franklin D. Roosevelt, for example, was paralyzed from the waist down as a result of polio. John F. Kennedy was a profligate womanizer who allegedly even carried on affairs in the White House. Even as recently as the 1980s, when Ronald Reagan was showing signs of Alzheimer's disease in his first term – his mental acuity was clearly failing, to the point that his staff had debated invoking the Twenty-fifth Amendment – the Washington press corps refused to report what they were seeing with their own eyes.

But that gentleman's agreement was tossed out the window for Bill Clinton.

Part of the reason for the change was that the entire media landscape had shifted. CNN had kicked off the 24-hour news cycle, and its ever-increasing demand for something to fill the airwaves, with its launch in 1980. Throughout that decade and into the 90s, so-called "tabloid TV" like Murdoch-owned *A Current Affair, Inside Edition* (hosted by Bill O'Reilly), and *Hard Copy* were capturing massive audiences with their sensationalized – and often poorly vetted – stories focused on sex, crime, and scandals. Like all beasts, they had to be fed, and subjects that were once considered off-limits or taboo were now fully in play.

The other, perhaps most important, factor in changing the media landscape was Reagan's gutting of the Fairness Doctrine in 1987. This regulation had required broadcasters to provide reasonably fair airtime for both sides of any controversial issues. The principle behind it was that since the airwaves belonged to everyone, if a company wanted to use those airwaves to make a profit, it needed to serve the public interest. "Commercial radio broadcasting was not, in other words, originally conceived as just another for-profit industry; it was supposed to meet a higher standard of social responsibility."[10]

But under Reagan, the very idea of "the public interest" was heresy to the free-market ideologues in his administration, and the once-public airwaves were turned over to private corporations. This directly led to one of the most far-reaching changes in the media landscape until the advent of social media: the rise in influence and popularity of AM talk radio.

Now unfettered by the bounds of the Fairness Doctrine, and motivated solely by how many listeners they could attract and sell to advertisers, a whole new kind of talk radio personality emerged: the shock jock. And no one exemplified this new breed of talk radio host than Rush Limbaugh, whose show debuted immediately following the repeal of the Fairness Doctrine. His hours-long live show consisted of his monologues about the news of the day, mostly ranting about feminists, liberals, and Democrats, with the occasional ad break and parody skit to break things up. His aggressive style and vitriolic name-calling became his signature – he would go on to coin the term "femi-nazis," label activist Sandra Fluke a "slut," and call Chelsea Clinton (who was only thirteen at the time) a dog.

Soon after his show's debut in 1988, bloviating Rush clones began colonizing the AM dial, spreading like kudzu, suffocating a once diverse ecosystem of voices and giving rise to an entire genre of right-wing talk shows that would see its apotheosis – or, more accurately, its nadir – in Alex Jones. Rush himself quickly became one of the right's most influential figures, to the point of being granted a Presidential Medal of Freedom by President Trump in 2020.

That level of discourse – the lies, name-calling, and attacks – in turn, influenced politicians, particularly in the Republican party. Around the same time Clinton was gearing up to run for president, a Republican Congress member named Newt Gingrich – financed by Richard Mellon Scaife, among others – was working on a bold political strategy.

Turning the old adage "all politics is local" upside down, he made all politics national, cultivating the hyper-partisan tribalism we have today. He worked to purge the moderates from the party by labeling them RINOs – Republicans In Name Only.

He also launched a movement to remake the way Republicans campaigned. While there had always been mudslinging in political races, Gingrich pushed it to a new level. In a memo circulated to fellow Republicans in 1990 titled "Language, a Key Mechanism of Control," he encouraged his colleagues to "be nasty," and start calling the opposition names like "sick," "corrupt," "anti-family," "degenerate," and "traitors" out to "destroy our country."[11,12] This new, nastier form of discourse, pioneered by the likes of Limbaugh and codified by Gingrich, became embedded in the Republican Party's DNA.

It was this toxic stew of media sensationalism and political rancor that Bill Clinton waded into with his first presidential campaign. Back home, the lieutenant governor, Jim Guy Tucker, was often left in charge as acting governor while Clinton was out on the campaign trail.

Tucker was a former high-school football player and college boxer who never outgrew his pugilistic character. Staffers characterized him as "abrupt and dictatorial ... meticulous and demanding," and "wouldn't take no for an answer." But they also said that he was extremely intelligent and could take in a lot of information quickly.[13]

Tucker was also an advocate for prison reform. In 1970, when he was the state attorney general, he created a fake identity – James Gus Turner – to go undercover at Cummins Prison, where he was able to very quickly bribe the trustees and get released. Though he was only there for thirty-six hours, the conditions there appalled him. He witnessed corruption, overcrowding, lack of food, and unhygienic conditions.[14]

And here is where we return to Wayne Dumond. By 1992, Dusty, the Hills, and Jay Cole had been working on his behalf for years. Jack and Anne were, seemingly, pushing the theory that Wayne was only convicted because of Coolidge Conlee's corruption, and was only being denied clemency because of Bill Clinton's relationship with the victim.

But Dusty and Jay were going down a slightly different track. Perhaps Jay influenced Dusty's thinking – or maybe they both influenced each other. But their theory put more of the responsibility for Wayne's incarceration not on Clinton's bias against him, but on an ever-more conspiratorial belief that Clinton was actually directly responsible for Wayne's castration as well as his "unjust" conviction. Through Cole's radio show and his connection to the Arkansas Baptist State Convention – the state's largest organization, with nearly half a million members – he agitated for Wayne's cause, painting him as an innocent victim, attacked and mutilated, then thrown in prison, on behalf of that morally bankrupt, anti-American, Communist-sympathizing Democrat, Bill Clinton.

They turned out letter-writing campaigns to public officials and newspapers (including the sympathetic *Arkansas Democrat*, run by Clinton critic Bob Starr). Most of these letters emphasized both the brutality of the castration – many implying, or outright stating, that Clinton himself was responsible for it – and that Wayne was innocent, based on Moses Schanfield's tainted tests. So, while Wayne's case wasn't exactly the number one controversy in Arkansas, plenty of people were aware of it, and if they only read about it in the opinion pages of their local papers, they probably bought the tale that he was an innocent man and should be pardoned, or at least granted a new trial.

Maybe Jim Guy Tucker's short time in Cummins made him more sympathetic to Wayne's plight. But he was definitely moved by Wayne's castration, because in 1992, while Clinton was away campaigning and Tucker was acting governor, he caved to public pressure and reduced Dumond's sentence to a little over thirty-nine years. He said he had done so because the jury at Wayne's trial had not been allowed to take his castration into account – a wise decision on Judge Yates' part, recognizing that it would only bias the jury in his favor. And, indeed, it had certainly biased plenty of people outside the courtroom – including Acting Governor Tucker – in his favor.

Even shortened, Wayne's sentence was still a long one. But importantly, this change meant he would one day be eligible for parole – and one more step closer to freedom.

***

Despite the number of factors working against him, Bill Clinton won the 1992 presidential election. In December of that year, he officially resigned as governor of Arkansas, and Jim Guy Tucker was elevated to acting governor, at least until a special election could determine who would fill both the governor's and lieutenant governor's seats.

Sheffield Nelson threw his hat in the ring again, this time against Tucker running to win the seat for real. Tucker won, handily, with nearly sixty percent of the vote.

The lieutenant governor's race was much tighter. Democrat Nate Coulter ran against Republican Mike Huckabee, a former Baptist minister fresh off a failed U.S. Senate campaign. Asa Hutchinson, the head of the state's RNC (and future governor himself), urged Huckabee to just pivot his senatorial campaign to run for lieutenant governor. So Huckabee ran, and won – barely, by only about 5,000 votes – thanks to the support of the newly energized Evangelical vote, served up by none other than Jay Cole.

ENDNOTES:

1. Associated Press, "Clinton Decides He Won't Seek '88 Nomination," *The New York Times*, July 15, 1987.

2. Ernest Dumas, "Bill Clinton," *Encyclopedia of Arkansas*.

3. David Maraniss, "Before Race Began, Clinton Resolved Pledge Not to Run," *The Washington Post*, July 14, 1992.

4. Joe Conason and Gene Lyons, *The Hunting of the President: The Ten-Year Campaign to Destroy Bill and Hillary Clinton* (New York, New York: St. Martin's Press, 2000), p. 3.

5. Conason and Lyons, *The Hunting of the President,* p. 9.

6. Conason and Lyons, *The Hunting of the President,* p. 9.

7. Conason and Lyons, *The Hunting of the President,* p. 10.

8. Conason and Lyons, *The Hunting of the President,* p. 9.

9. Gene Lyons, "The roots of the Clinton smear," *Salon.com*, February 5, 1998.

10. "Overview: The Rise of Talk Radio," PBS.org, July 12, 2005.

11. Michael D'Antonio, *The Hunting of Hillary*, (Thomas Dunne Books: New York, New York, 2020), p. 4.

12. "The Politics of Slash and Burn," *The New York Times* Opinion, September 20, 1990.

13. Robert L. Brown, "Jim Guy Tucker," *Defining Moments: Historic Decisions by Arkansas Governors from McMath through Huckabee* (Fayetteville, Arkansas: The University of Arkansas Press) 2010, p. 112.

14. "Arkansas Prison Reform," *The James Guy Tucker, Jr., Processing Blog.* Center for Arkansas History and Culture, December 22, 2015.

Chapter 8: The Arkansas Project

Only one week before Arkansas' 1993 special election, one of the most tragic events in the Clinton saga transpired: the body of Vince Foster, long-time Clinton friend and deputy White House counsel, was found in a park outside of Washington, D.C., dead from a self-inflicted gunshot wound.

Immediately on the heels of that event, Rush Limbaugh helped launch the longest-lasting, most damaging conspiracy theory in America. He told his millions of listeners that Foster's death was not by his own hand, but on the orders of Hillary Clinton. According to Rush, Foster "knew something" about Hillary's Whitewater dealings – something that she was willing to kill to keep quiet.

Much less publicly, but maybe even more consequentially, the day after Foster's body was found, four men went on a boat trip in the Chesapeake Bay: Emmett Tyrrell Jr., the founder and editor-in-chief of the right-wing magazine *American Spectator*; Richard Larry, a senior aide to media mogul Richard Mellon Scaife (the *Spectator*'s major financier); public relations consultant and *Spectator* board member David W. Henderson; and Washington attorney and conservative activist Steven Boynton. From this trip, the Arkansas Project was born.[1]

Several books have been written (and at least two documentaries filmed) on this sprawling, tragicomic operation; *The Hunting of the President* by Joe Conason and Gene Lyons is an excellent source, along with the two documentaries based on it. In a nutshell, the Arkansas Project was a secretive, loosely coordinated smear campaign against the Clintons financed by Scaife to the tune of more than $2 million. The basic playbook was for his operatives in Arkansas to recruit sources to find any dirt they could on the Clintons – verifiable or not. Those allegations would then be picked up by the *American Spectator* and other right-wing tabloids like the *Washington Times* and the *New York Post*. The "eyes and ears" of the Arkansas Project were sex-obsessed anti-Clinton crackpots Everett Ham, head of a conservative group dedicated to taking down Clinton, and Parker Dozhier, a friend of Boynton's and a paranoid gun nut who was convinced the "Clinton machine" was out to kill him.

According to David Brock in his book *Blinded by the Right: The Conscience of an Ex-Conservative*, the political culture in Arkansas was "a hotbed of conspiracy and lunacy" where "making up stories about one's political enemies – the more lascivious and bizarre the better – was something of a political tradition."[2]

So Ham and Dozier were easily able to recruit a cast of questionable "sources," including Gene Wirges, a former muckraker who believed Clinton's anti-war protests were treason (and petitioned the State of Missouri to disqualify Clinton from the ballot on those grounds); Larry Nichols, the former ADFA official who got caught using state resources to aid the Iran-Contra affair; as well as disgruntled state police troopers, former business associates, and anyone else with a grudge against Bill or Hillary. These "sources" were secretly funneled money for any "inside scoops" they could provide – whether they were true or not. Thanks to the efforts of the Arkansas Project, every rumor and conspiracy theory about the Clintons was dug up – or outright invented – including any number of "preposterous accusations that the Clintons were involved in everything from sex orgies to drug-running to murder."[3]

First there was "Troopergate," kicked off with a novella-length piece written by Brock for the *American Spectator* in late 1993. Titled "His Cheatin' Heart," the hit piece repeats allegations from four former state troopers who claimed they'd helped Bill arrange for dozens of sexual trysts. Salon columnist Amanda Marcotte describes it most accurately as "a true masterpiece of right-wing agitprop, simultaneously leering and judgmental."[4] In it, Brock portrays Bill as "sexually incontinent white trash"[5] and Hillary as a "foul-mouthed, castrating, power-mad harpy."[6]

That story made a huge splash on the national scene. The *Washington Post* picked it up, of course, as well as CNN and the *LA Times*, who even flew the former troopers out to Los Angeles. None of them did any real fact-checking on the troopers' claims. The "news angle" that each of them used to justify publishing the allegations was ostensibly about Clinton's misuse of government resources – i.e., the troopers' time and patrol cars – and his alleged promises of cushy federal jobs in return for their silence. But it was clear that the salacious details were really the whole point.

These stories, in turn, spawned any number of copycats – nearly anyone who had lived in Arkansas and had a tale of Bill Clinton's sex life was catapulted to the front pages of the supermarket tabloids – and, often, paid handsomely for it. One disgruntled former state trooper claimed he'd helped Bill arrange for hundreds of trysts – a physical impossibility, considering the brief length of time he'd been employed. A rumor that Clinton had fathered a "love child" with a Black woman was splashed across the front pages of the seamier tabloids – even after a DNA test disproved it.

Nearly all of these stories fell apart under investigation. The original Troopergate allegations – both the sexual encounters and the "hush-money" offers – were eventually recanted by the troopers under oath. It would later be revealed that they held grudges against Bill for not bringing them to Washington with him, and one of them had even considered blackmailing him with the allegations. More importantly, they had been paid tens of thousands of dollars by Arkansas Project operatives as well as Peter W. Smith, a Chicago investment banker and major donor to GOPAC who had spent at least $80,000 to investigate Bill's sex life.[7]

Despite the sex scandals not really having any "there" there, one scandal in particular did stick – and turn into one of the biggest scandals of any presidency up to that point. In the original Troopergate story, Brock had contacted the women the troopers had named as having had sex with Bill. The women all either denied the allegations or refused to speak to Brock. So he decided to leave their names out of his story.

That is, except for one, a woman the troopers just named "Paula." Brock said he figured since they had only used her first name, she wasn't actually being identified. So he left it in.

According to Danny Ferguson, one of the former troopers, in May of 1991, Bill had rented a room at the Excelsior in downtown Little Rock after he'd given a speech there. Ferguson said Bill had told him to tell the woman, "Paula," that she "made his knees knock" and to bring her to his room. Ferguson said he did so, then waited outside the room. Less than an hour later, according to Ferguson, Paula emerged from the room and told him that she was willing to be Bill's "regular girlfriend."[8]

The woman turned out to be former ADFA employee Paula Jones (who went by Corbin at the time). In the wake of the Troopergate story, she filed suit against Clinton for sexual harassment in May of 1994, just two days before the statute of limitations was about to run out. In it, she alleged that

Ferguson had indeed brought her up to Clinton's room at the Excelsior, where he caressed and kissed her, then exposed himself to her and told her to "kiss it." She said she left the room then, and she denies Ferguson's claim that she said she was willing to be his girlfriend.

In her suit – funded and supported by Scaife and other right-wing power players, including legal advisers like the anti-abortion activist Susan Carpenter McMillan and others from the Federalist Society – she asked for $700,000.

Her case, however, was on shaky ground; one U.S. Circuit Court judge had summarily dismissed it because of lack of evidence. Indeed, testimony from people around her at the time painted her as a Clinton "groupie" who would "hang out in the hotel lobby to catch a glimpse" of him.[9] But thanks to having such a well-funded legal team, she was able to keep appealing.

Clinton, understandably, wanted to postpone the trial, arguing that dealing with a civil trial while serving in office would place undue burden on a sitting president. That case went up to the Supreme Court, which issued a landmark, unanimous ruling that sitting presidents were not immune from being sued in civil court.

It was in his depositions for this case – broadcast on national TV – that he perjured himself in denying he had sex with his intern Monica Lewinsky. It was that perjury – lying to cover up a sexual affair - that would ultimately be the basis for his impeachment.

Clinton had offered to settle the lawsuit for the entire $700,000, but Carpenter McMillan advised Jones to refuse the offer and hold out for the entire amount plus a public apology. In November 1998, Clinton agreed to a settlement of $850,000.

***

But far worse than the sexual infidelity allegations, the Arkansas Project worked to throw more doubt on Vince Foster's suicide, even though he had left a suicide note and had been being treated for depression – thanks to being one of the innocent targets of the anti-Clinton smear machine.

Foster's suicide was quickly – and wrongfully – linked to the emerging Whitewater scandal, with the claim that because Foster had been in possession of the Rose Law Firm's billing records about the Whitewater deal, he allegedly knew "the truth" about the deal and was killed in order to silence him.

But what was Whitewater, exactly? The term comes from the Whitewater Development Corporation, a company formed in 1978 by Bill, Hillary, and their friends Jim and Susan McDougal. Under the company's name, they borrowed $203,000 to buy 230 acres of remote land in the Ozarks with the plan of selling lots for vacation homes. But when interest rates skyrocketed, the real-estate market plunged, and the four lost most of their investment.[10]

Jim McDougal later acquired a small bank and a small savings and loan company in 1980 and 1982, respectively. They – along with many others – collapsed in the national savings and loan crisis of the 1980s.[11] Though these deals had nothing to do with the Clintons, they would become important facts in the overall Whitewater scandal.

Though Jim was tried and acquitted on charges of bank fraud in connection with the failed savings and loan, he was bitter because he felt like the Clintons hadn't defended him during the trial, and that he had borne more of the financial risk with Whitewater than the Clintons had.

Perhaps more importantly, his legal problems had exacerbated his mental illness – he had tried to get out of his 1990 trial by pleading insanity – so he ended up broke and living on Social Security. He had repeatedly asked the governor's office to give him a job, to no avail. Clinton aides had warned that Jim was reckless and couldn't be trusted. In fact, Beverly Bassett Schaffer, a Clinton-appointed securities commissioner, had asked the FBI to investigate his business dealings.[12]

The Clintons had been distancing themselves from him because of his increasingly erratic behavior – not to mention the fact that it was his mismanagement of Whitewater Development Corp's finances that contributed to its collapse.

Jim's bitterness grew into a thirst for revenge. So he reached out to one of his other old business partners (and Clinton opponent) Sheffield Nelson, to recruit him into getting back at Clinton. Nelson, in turn, reached out to *New York Times* reporter Jeff Gerth, who had noticed the term "Whitewater" on some of the Clintons' financial records and was looking for an Arkansas source for that story. Nelson gave him Jim's number.[13]

Gerth drove down to Arkansas and met with Jim, who gave him documents and canceled checks that he alleged showed the Clintons had cut some legal corners with their Whitewater finances, such as taking improper tax deductions and not paying their fair share of Whitewater's expenses.[14]

Gerth's piece ran on the front page of the *Times* in March of 1992. The story never directly states what crimes the Clintons allegedly committed, but it was more of a stew of innuendos designed to imply that something shady was going on with the Clintons in Whitewater. Gene Lyons summarized the Whitewater allegations like this: "When he was governor, Clinton and his wife entered into a sweetheart deal with a crooked financier at no risk to themselves. When their benefactor got into trouble, Clinton dumped the sitting Arkansas securities commissioner and appointed a political ally named Beverly Bassett Schaffer. He and Hillary then pressured Bassett Schaffer to grant special favors to Madison [Guaranty Savings and Loan, owned by Jim McDougal], until vigilant federal regulators cracked down and thwarted their scheme."[15]

Problem was, absolutely none of that was true. But because it had been printed in the *Times*, it had the stamp of legitimacy and was treated as gospel by the mainstream media and the public at large. The "questions" and vague innuendos of wrongdoing soon became near-daily stories in the news media.

Then, adding fuel to the fire, the day after Foster committed suicide, the FBI raided the offices of Judge David Hale. According to Max Brantley, Hale was "known as a serial liar, involved in any number of sleazy deals." He'd been getting away with various scams for years, but in July 1993, it was all about to come crashing down.[16] Hale was facing indictment for embezzling more than $2 million in federally backed small-business loans, and, as Brantley put it, he was willing to do anything to make it go away.[17] So, as a ploy to get the heat off himself, he offered to enter a plea deal where he would implicate Bill Clinton by claiming that Clinton had pressured him into making an illegal loan to Susan McDougal, wife of Jim McDougal, in connection with the Whitewater deal.

Boynton and Henderson began spending a lot of time with Hale in secretive locations in Arkansas – including a "safe house" owned by Dozhier – and Hale's allegations, though they were never substantiated, were frequently published in the *Spectator*.[18] Many suspected that some of the Arkansas Project money was being funneled to Hale.[19]

In addition to promoting Hale's allegations in the *Spectator*, Scaife hired Christopher Ruddy, a writer at the *New York Post* who had first insinuated that the Clintons were involved in Foster's death (Ruddy would later go on to become CEO of Newsmax). His new job was to dig into those allegations and keep them on the front page of another Scaife publication, *The Pittsburgh Tribune-Review*.

But it wasn't just Scaife and the Arkansas Project digging into the failed land deal; Citizens United, a conservative media-advocacy group, hired David Bossie as a full-time investigator to dig up dirt on the Clintons and Whitewater.[20] That "dirt" – true or not – would then be published in Citizen United's *ClintonWatch* newsletter and passed on to the many journalists who used Citizens United as a source.

Those stories would then become part of the circular, incestuous pipeline of right-wing bullshit. The *American Spectator, ClintonWatch, The Washington Times*, and other right-wing publications would use Ruddy's articles and Bossie's "tips" as sources for their own stories about the Clintons' supposed criminal enterprises.[21] Opinion columnists in otherwise respected newspapers – like William Safire of *The New York Times* – would opine on all the "questions raised" about Foster's death and/or the Whitewater deal, based on nothing but the speculations and wild allegations printed in the right-wing propaganda rags – thereby boosting them into respectability.

Those articles and columns, in turn, would be read and discussed uncritically on right-wing talk shows like Rush Limbaugh, who embellished the conspiracy theory by stating Foster was murdered in an apartment owned by Hillary. Roger Ailes himself appeared on *The Don Imus Show* to promote Ruddy's work and push the theory that Foster had been murdered.

And of course, the right-wing fundamentalists, who already believed the Clintons were practically Satan incarnate, picked it up as well. Pat Robertson dedicated an entire episode of *The 700 Club* to Foster's death, titled "Suicide or Murder?"

Then there was *The Clinton Chronicles*, a "documentary" that was released straight to VHS in 1994. It was actually a reboot/sequel of an earlier "documentary" called *Clinton's Circle of Power*. Both were produced by Pat Matrisciana and funded by Larry Nichols, Jerry Falwell, Jay Cole, and others under the organization "Citizens for Honest Government."

The Clinton Chronicles, partially narrated by Nichols, paints Bill Clinton as though he was some uber-mafioso who ran Arkansas like his own personal fiefdom, recycling every wild allegation and conspiracy theory about the Clintons. It alleges that Bill was somehow involved in money laundering, drug smuggling, and gun running through the Mena airport (a conspiracy theory that had originally blamed the CIA under Reagan). It also accuses him of several other criminal activities – including the Wirges allegation that he "did business" in Moscow "against the United States government."

It also places Foster's death into the "Clinton Body Count" conspiracy theory. The Clinton Body Count likely started around 1993 as a blog/website run by Linda Thompson, a pro-gun-rights lawyer. On her site, she listed two dozen people – including Foster – who were connected to the Clintons and had suffered a sudden death by accident, homicide, or suicide, even decades after their supposed involvement with them.

Thompson was also part of the growing anti-government, right-wing militia movement. While it had gotten its start in the 1980s, the movement was turbo-charged by Clinton's election. First, his support for the Brady Bill, which would ban the manufacture, sale, or possession of semiautomatic weapons, riled up the Second Amendment absolutists and likely drove up recruitment into militias.

But even more than that, the tragic events at Ruby Ridge, Idaho, and Waco, Texas, activated them to do more than just pay membership dues and stockpile AK-47s.

The standoff at Ruby Ridge went down in August 1992, under George H.W. Bush's presidency. Federal law enforcement agents had been dispatched to serve an arrest warrant on Randy Weaver, a white supremacist militia type, setting off an eleven-day standoff. During the standoff, law enforcement agents killed Weaver's wife and oldest son. Because of the federal agents' mistakes and general flubbing of the operation, many people – not just militia types – were shocked and horrified at law enforcement's actions. The militia types, though, went ballistic.

Then, only three months after Clinton's inauguration, there was the Waco siege. This time the Bureau of Alcohol, Tobacco, and Firearms was there to serve an arrest warrant for illegal weapons, and a search warrant for potential child sex abuse, on the Branch Davidian cult leader, David Koresh. The armed stand-off lasted fifty-one days before the entire compound went up in flames, killing eighty people, including children. To this day, it's unclear who actually caused the fire, but anti-government groups immediately pinned the blame on law enforcement. It became the "bloody shirt" they waved to incite anti-government sentiment – and actions. Among the many people radicalized by the Waco siege was Gulf War veteran and white supremacist Timothy McVeigh, who would, two years later, commit the deadliest act of domestic terrorism on American soil.

Thompson's website was just one small part of this rabid anti-government movement. It was promoted through the same pre-internet militia movement that McVeigh traveled in: flyers and bumper stickers handed out at gun shows and letters to the editors of right-wing newsletters and magazines. Soon, it was picked up by an untold number of right-wing talk radio hosts, political opponents, online BBS posters – then in a well-funded "documentary" being promoted and sold on Jerry Falwell's *Old Time Gospel Hour*.

The producers said they sold 300,000 copies of *The Clinton Chronicles*, though some sources say that many of these were bulk purchases by right-wing organizations, who would then give them away.

***

Thanks to the near-constant drumbeat of criminal allegations in the press, in the wake of David Hale's allegations, Clinton caved to public pressure and instructed then-Attorney General Janet Reno to name a special prosecutor to investigate Whitewater and the death of Vince Foster.

The first special prosecutor she appointed was Robert Fiske, a well-respected moderate Republican and the former U.S. attorney for the Southern District of New York. He conducted an investigation and released his preliminary report in June of 1994. In it, he absolved the Clintons of any wrongdoing and ruled Foster's death a suicide.

But for Republicans in Congress, that simply would not do. Besides opening Congressional hearings into Whitewater, they pressured the special panel tasked with appointing an independent council to oust Fiske (the law had just changed so that now a special three-judge panel appointed an independent council, rather than the attorney general appointing a special prosecutor).

The panel itself was composed of judges appointed, directly or indirectly, by rabid right-winger Jesse Helms. The head of the panel, John Sentelle, had been appointed by Reagan at the urging of Jesse Helms. He was also the judge who had overturned the convictions in the Iran-Contra affair.

This panel then named Kenneth Starr as the new independent council in August 1994. Far from being a neutral, fair-minded investigator, Starr was a known Republican operative and had even provided legal advice to Paula Jones.

Starr's Whitewater investigation would become the longest, most expensive independent council in American history, lasting a total of eight years and costing anywhere from $50 million to $70 million. As it dragged on, it succumbed to "mission bloat," straying far afield from its original task of investigating any potential crimes associated with Whitewater or Foster's death. After failing to find enough evidence of criminality in either, Starr (and his deputy, Brett Kavanaugh) began looking into Bill Clinton's sex life. Despite having the immense resources of the FBI at his disposal, Starr began paying private detectives – who weren't under the same legal and ethical constraints as federal law enforcement agents – to dig up any dirt they could find. Anyone associated with the Clintons, no matter how distantly or innocuously, was strong-armed in what Max Brantley called "scary, police-state kind of tactics."[22]Since the full scope of the Whitewater scandal and investigation is far too wide and complex to cover here (again, I highly recommend Conason's and Lyons' book if you want to get the full story), I will attempt to focus only on the parts of the scandal that affected the fate of Wayne Dumond. And that is where we come to the sad fate of Gov. Jim Guy Tucker.

Jim McDougal and Tucker had several business entanglements, including shared ownership of the small bank McDougal had purchased in 1980 that later went bankrupt. Just before McDougal's fraud trial in 1990, Tucker learned that McDougal had collected loan payments from buyers on some land the two owned, but never gave the money to the bank. Instead, McDougal drew up fake deeds to give to the buyers and forged Tucker's signature on them. Tucker was subsequently forced to make restitution.[23]

In 1995, Starr had attempted to indict Tucker on bankruptcy fraud charges, based almost entirely on confessed embezzler David Hale's word. The charges were that Tucker, Jim and Susan McDougal, and David Hale had conspired to engage in fraudulent real estate deals to raise money for Hale's company. In other words, Tucker conspired to defraud the government of money so that he could then borrow it and pay interest on it. Which, of course, makes no sense.

U.S. District Court Judge Henry Woods (who had presided over Wayne's trial) had thrown the case out on the grounds that Tucker was not a "covered person" under the Independent Counsel Act, therefore not under Starr's jurisdiction, and that his alleged offenses were not related to Whitewater, the Clintons, Jim McDougal, or David Hale.

But Starr appealed that decision to the Eighth District Court of Appeals, and an all-Republican panel of judges reversed that decision, paving the way for Tucker to be tried, along with the McDougals.

The new judge in the case made several pre-trial rulings in favor of the prosecution. The first was to deny Tucker's motion to sever his trial from that of the McDougals. Another was to deny his motion to compel Starr to disclose any arrangements – financial or otherwise – his office or the FBI had made with Hale. And finally, they denied his request to see the FBI's raw notes of the more than forty meetings it had with Hale, instead only allowing Tucker's defense one document summarizing those meetings.[24]

Through the course of the trial, four of the charges against Tucker were dropped. In the end, the jury deliberated for nearly two weeks before coming back with their verdicts. Jim McDougal was convicted on eighteen courts of conspiracy and fraud and was sentenced to five years in prison, with two years suspended. Susan was found guilty of four counts of misusing SBA funds and making false statements in connection with a loan, and was sentenced to two years in prison. Jim Guy Tucker was found guilty of one count of conspiracy and one count of mail fraud, for making false statements on a loan form which had actually been prepared by Hale.[25] He was, in the end, sentenced to four years of probation.

In Arkansas, convicted felons are barred from holding office. So, in the wake of his conviction, Tucker announced he would resign as governor effective July 15, 1996. "Although I am innocent of the charges made," he said, "I must accept the verdict of the jury while I appeal."[26]

His resignation meant handing the keys to the governor's office to the newly elected lieutenant governor, Mike Huckabee.

1. Ernest Dumas, "Arkansas Project," *The Encyclopedia of Arkansas*, March 15, 2024.

2. David Brock, *Blinded by the Right: The Conscience of an Ex-Conservative* (New York, New York: Three Rivers Press, 2003) p. 214.

3. Brock, *Blinded by the Right*.

4. Amanda Marcotte, "The Clinton BS files: The right wing's long history of obsession with the Clintons' sex lives," Salon.com, August 22, 2016.

5. Marcotte, "Clinton BS."

6. Brock, *Blinded by the Right*, p. 165.

7. Murray Waas, "Arkansas trooper considered demanding money from President Clinton," Salon.com, April 9, 1998.

8. Brock, *Blinded by the Right*, p. 166.

9. Joe Conason, Gene Lyons, and Nickolas Perry, *The Hunting of the President*, directed by Nickolas Perry and Harry Thomason (2004; Los Angeles, California: Regent Releasing), Amazon Prime Video.

10. Ernest Dumas, "Whitewater Scandal," *The Encyclopedia of Arkansas*, July 29, 2024.

11. Dumas, "Whitewater Scandal."

12. Conason and Lyons, *Hunting of the President*, p. 31.

13. Conason and Lyons, *Hunting of the President*, p. 33.

14. Conason and Lyons, *Hunting of the President*.

15. Conason and Lyons, *Hunting of the President*, p. 34.

16. Perry and Thomason, *Hunting of the President*.

17. Perry and Thomason, *Hunting of the President*.

18. Brock, *Blinded by the Right*, p. 212.

19. Brock, *Blinded by the Right.*

20. Russell Watson, "Vince Foster's Suicide: The Rumor Mill Churns," *Newsweek*, March 20, 1994. Updated March 13, 2010.

21. Brock, *Blinded by the Right*, p. 219.

22. Perry and Thomason, *Hunting of the President.*

23. Conason and Lyons, *Hunting of the President*, p. 32.

24. Conason and Lyons, *Hunting of the President*, p. 222.

25. Conason and Lyons, *Hunting of the President*, p. 244.

26. Conason and Lyons, *Hunting of the President*, pp. 244-245.

Chapter 9: Mike Huckabee, Pastor-in-Chief

In his memoir *Character IS the Issue*, Mike Huckabee describes the tumultuous events of his inauguration on July 15, 1996, in great detail. He says he began the day, a brutally hot Monday, with a prayer and dedication service at the First Baptist Church in Little Rock, which he says felt "almost like an ordination."[1]

That afternoon, he went to his office in the capitol building and rehearsed the speech he planned to give that evening, after his inauguration. He finished his final practice speech at 1:55 p.m., only five minutes before the official swearing-in ceremony was scheduled.

Huckabee says he was stretching his legs when his phone rang – it was Governor Tucker. After a few moments of awkward chit-chat, Tucker dropped a bomb: "I wanted to let you know I've decided not to resign," he said, stating he had filed an appeal, and that until the court ruled on it, he decided to stay in office.[2]

Tucker had made the sudden, last-minute reversal because he had just learned a critical fact about his case: one of the jurors was tainted. The woman, Renee Johnson Hayes, was married to a man who had been convicted on drug charges, and Tucker, as acting governor, had twice refused to commute his sentence. Johnson Hayes hadn't spoken up when, during jury selection, the potential jury pool was asked if any of them had been affected by Tucker's actions as governor.[3]

That same man – the juror's husband – was also a relative of local restaurateur, philanthropist, "sweet potato pie king," and wing-nut Black activist Robert "Say" McIntosh. Say was well known in and around Little Rock for pulling outrageous protest stunts like tying himself to a cross (and nearly dying of heatstroke because of it), releasing truckloads of farm animals in various locations around the city, and attempting to cut down a tree dedicated to Martin Luther King, Jr.

He was also short-tempered and prone to violence. In 1983, he shot an accused domestic abuser in the ass, and in 1990, he punched a political candidate with ties to the KKK – then swore at his trial that the whole thing had been a stunt that he and his victim had mutually planned.[4]

Say was also well known for his hatred of Bill Clinton. He had bird-dogged Clinton during his presidential campaign and had promoted the accusation that he'd fathered a "love child" with a Black sex worker.

But more importantly, Say had been a regular protester at the Tucker-McDougal trial, passing out "luridly illustrated" flyers accusing Tucker of crimes and "immoral acts."[5] Say had been at the courthouse in May, on the day the verdicts were announced. When the crew from CNN attempted to film a live shot on the courthouse steps, Say kept disrupting the shot. So when the producer tried to get him out of the way, Say punched the producer out, earning himself an assault conviction.

Anyway, during the time Say had been protesting at the trial, he had bragged that he "had one on the jury." And unlike a lot of the things that came out of Say's mouth, this one was actually true.

When he learned about this, Tucker, still a fighter, immediately moved to have his conviction overturned on that basis. Tucker's friends said he agonized over his resignation that whole weekend and into the day Monday. He reportedly drafted two letters, one, the unqualified resignation, and another, where he only claimed a temporary disability and granted Huckabee power as acting governor until Tucker could overturn his conviction.[6]

Huckabee says that during that phone call, he tried to convince Tucker to rethink his decision, unsuccessfully.

While the House chambers were filling up, and the live TV coverage had already begun, Tucker sent a letter to both Huckabee and the state legislature reiterating his decision not to resign. He also held a press conference of his own, explaining his decision to withdraw his resignation. As he walked out of the state capitol building afterwards, crowds of Huckabee supporters booed and yelled insults at him.

Tucker's change of mind sparked a state constitutional crisis: now, who was the actual governor? The scene at the Capitol building devolved into chaos. The crowds that had gathered for Huckabee's swearing in – including both state and national media – were a mass of confusion and loud disarray. No one really knew what was going on or what to do.

Huckabee made the decision that since Tucker's original resignation had been set for noon, that meant that at that moment, he, Huckabee, was the governor, until and unless the courts decided otherwise. He called up several Democrats and urged them to meet with Tucker and convince him to step down, for the good of the state. And if he wouldn't do so voluntarily, he would face impeachment. Tucker, unsurprisingly, remained defiant.

It was only after state Attorney General Winston Bryant (also a Democrat) filed an emergency lawsuit to force him out, did Tucker finally back down with a short, handwritten letter to the president pro tempore of the senate: "Dear Mr. President: This is to inform you that I hereby resign the office of the governor effective at 6:00 p.m. July 15, 1996." Thus, after four hours of confusion and chaos, the dust settled, and Mike Huckabee was sworn in as Arkansas' forty-fourth governor.

To understand Mike Huckabee, you have to understand him in relation to Bill Clinton, because nearly everything Huckabee does or says is because of, or in direct response to, Clinton. They were both born in Hope, Arkansas, and went to the same school, albeit nine years apart. They both play musical instruments: Bill, (famously) the saxophone, and Mike, the bass guitar. Both are outgoing and friendly; they love campaigning and exude what the press likes to call "folksy charm."

Maybe more consequentially, both participated in the VFW's Boys' State program, which inspired both of them to pursue careers in politics – though on opposite sides of the aisle. In fact, Huckabee fully admits that his conservatism was a direct backlash to Clinton's – and his peers' – progressivism.

Though Huckabee and Clinton hail from the same hometown, their childhoods differed in a few important ways. Despite being nearly a decade older than Huckabee, Clinton was born to a single mom and lived in the kind of multi-generational blended family that is now much more accepted.

Huckabee, on the other hand, had the kind of traditional, two-parent, heterosexual family Evangelicals insist on. But the Huckabee household wasn't exactly Ozzie and Harriet; his father worked two jobs, as a mechanic and a firefighter, and his mother worked as a clerk, struggling to make ends meet. Neither of them had graduated high school, and they had come from the kind of poverty you only find in the deepest rural areas; his mother grew up in a cabin with dirt floors and no running water.[7]

Like most Arkansans at the time, his family were Democrats, and in his youth, he identified as one as well, more out of habit than anything. His first job, though, changed that. He was only fourteen years old when local radio magnate Haskell Jones gave him a job as an announcer at KXAR radio. Huckabee describes Haskell as a "patriot" who "loved America," and one of the few Republicans in the state at the time. When Haskell took over KXAR, he had changed the station's format from the typical small-town AM station programming, broadcasting news and hit music, to one more religiously focused. He even had ministers broadcast shows live from the studio on Sunday mornings.[8]

Huckabee says that Haskell taught him that America's freedoms and economic prosperity were blessings that came from God, not the government, a belief that would become a founding principle for most of the militia movement. Haskell also gave Huckabee a book, *A Choice Not an Echo*, by Phyllis Schlafly – the book that inspired both Barry Goldwater and a young Huckabee.[9]

Huckabee says that he came of age during that time, the late 1960s, "when this country was literally burning with riots and descent," as he put it in a speech to CPAC. The same Democratic National Convention where Hillary Rodham had witnessed police brutality against protestors, inspiring her to leave her parents' party and become a Democrat, Mike Huckabee saw – from his studio booth 750 miles away – as "mayhem" that inspired him to leave his parents' party and become a Republican. Huckabee would write in his memoir, *Character IS the Issue* (the title itself a direct rebuke to Bill Clinton allegedly saying that "character isn't the issue"), "We lived in the age of the birth control pill, free love, gay sex, the drug culture, and reckless disregard for standards" and that this "gave personal debauchery a new license."[10]

Then, the events of the summer of 1972 would plant the roots of his two life missions, religion and politics, even deeper.

In June of that year, he attended Explo '72, the first worldwide gathering hosted by Campus Crusade for Christ, an ultra-conservative Evangelical organization. On the last night of the conference, he heard its founder, Rev. Billy Graham, speak to 100,000 people at the Cotton Bowl in Dallas. His message, "You can touch the world. One person can make a difference," inspired Huckabee deeply.[11] Graham, of course, would go on to become one of the most powerful Evangelicals in politics, serving as a sort of unofficial White House pastor until his health began failing during Obama's first term. Scarcely a month after getting fired up by Graham's speech, Huckabee attended Boys' State, where he was elected "governor" of his state's delegates. The connections he made there paved the way for him to be recruited by Nixon's re-election campaign to serve as their south Arkansas youth coordinator – right around the same time that Hillary was assisting the Watergate Committee in its investigation of Nixon.[12]

Huckabee graduated high school a year later, the first one in his family to do so. He then went on to study religion and speech at Ouachita Baptist University in south Arkansas. He graduated early, in 1975, but not before marrying his high-school sweetheart, Janet. After that, he attended the Southwestern Baptist Theological Seminary in Fort Worth, Texas.

Once out of college, he was hired as communications director for yet another archconservative, the televangelist

James Robison. In August of 1980, as a member of his staff, Huckabee helped Robison organize the fateful Freedom Rally in Dallas that was attended by tens of thousands of Evangelical Christians. The speaker list was a who's-who of all the big-name Evangelicals, including Jerry Falwell, Pat Robertson, and Phyllis Schlafly.

It was at this rally where, in his warm-up for then-candidate Ronald Reagan, Robison urged Christians to "crawl out from under the pews and stop looking through stained-glass windows" and instead get involved in politics to "take over this country."

"I'm sick and tired of hearing about all of the *radicals*, and the *perverts*, and the *liberals*, and the *leftists*, and the *Communists* coming out of the closet," he preached with fire-and-brimstone intensity. "It's time for *God's people* to come out of the closet!"

Then Reagan came onstage, where he began his speech with the famous lines: "I know you can't endorse me … but I want you to know that I endorse you and what you are doing."

This rally is really where the Moral Majority movement was born, and it is widely acknowledged as "the single most important religio-political moment in modern American life,"[13] when Evangelicals embraced and merged with the Republican Party. Robison credits that rally with reaching pastors across the nation, who then turned out their parishioners to vote for Reagan (and against the Baptist Sunday-school teacher Jimmy Carter), handing him the White House.

Even though some in the Christian press unironically called this rally Huckabee's "coming out party," Huckabee left Robison's staff shortly afterwards.

After that, Huckabee went on to pastor at Baptist churches in Pine Bluff and Texarkana. But from his time with Robison,

Huckabee gained an appreciation for television, which he called "the most powerful tool in history."[14] To that end, he would film his sermons each Sunday, then make copies of them on VHS to give out to anyone who had missed church.

But he had bigger ambitions. He founded small Christian TV stations in each city, and he launched a weekly Christian TV talk show called *Positive Alternatives*. While it wasn't exactly breaking the Nielson ratings, it was moderately popular among Evangelicals and other Christians in Arkansas.

It was through this religious media work that he met Jay Cole. In an article in *The Nation*, Cole said that when Huckabee launched his preaching career, he went straight to Cole for assistance.

Cole's Missionary Tape & Equipment Supply company had experience setting up Christian television and radio stations in the U.S. and abroad, so Cole said that when Huckabee started his own stations, he called on Cole for help.[15]

He apparently called on Cole's help later for another endeavor: in 1989, with Cole's support, Huckabee was named the youngest-ever president of the nearly 500,000-member Arkansas Baptist State Convention, one of the most powerful groups in the state at the time.

But Huckabee still had bigger ambitions. In his memoir, he says he believed he was always destined for politics,[16] so, in 1992, after twelve years as a pastor, he "felt God's call to leave the pulpit and take his message to the political arena."[17] He also recognized that leading the Arkansas Baptist State Convention was what paved the way for him to do so.

In his memoir, Huckabee says that many of his parishioners weren't happy with this decision. Most Christians, despite over a decade of lobbying by the Moral Majority, still didn't want to get involved with politics. Huckabee dismissed their concerns with one of his many homey little aphorisms: "Everybody wants to eat from a clean plate, but nobody wants to do the dishes."[18]

To Huckabee, apparently, Democrats were the filth that needed to be cleaned off the plate. He ran his campaign against incumbent U.S. Sen. Dale Bumpers, a moderate Democrat, using "a playbook straight out of James Dobson, [where] he tried to portray Bumpers as a pornographer for his support of federal grants to the arts."[19] When he was campaigning, he would push back against reluctant Christians by telling them that Democrats were "letting men marry men" and "killing unborn children"[20] – this during a wave of terrorist attacks and death threats against abortion providers across the nation.

The campaign of terror by the militant anti-abortion movement – which had significant overlap with the white supremacist militia movement – had continued into the '90s, with bombings, bomb threats, death threats, hate mail, and harassing phone calls escalating. Anti-abortion groups would doxx abortion providers using "Wanted" posters (both on paper and online), and some hosted what can only be called "hit lists" with names of abortion providers across the nation, with their names struck through if they were killed.

The year before Huckabee's run for the Senate had seen the anti-abortion movement's largest public action. The "Summer of Mercy," a forty-two-day siege of Wichita, Kansas, involved blockading clinics and threatening patients and doctors – especially Dr. George Tiller.

Dr. Tiller was one of the few doctors in the U.S. who performed late-term abortions and was one of the movement's main targets for violence. Right-wing pundits, including Rush Limbaugh and Bill O'Reilly, repeatedly called him "Tiller the baby killer."

Two years later, in 1993, an anti-abortion militant shot Dr. Tiller five times, nearly killing him (in 2009, he was assassinated inside his church). That same year, Dr. David Gunn was shot to death outside a clinic in Pensacola, Florida, and the following year, Dr. John Britton and his bodyguard, James Barrett, were shot to death in front of another clinic in Pensacola.

Many on the right either publicly condoned the violence, seeing it as justifiable in defense of saving unborn children, or else blamed "lone wolves" in an attempt to gaslight the public that their rabid anti-abortion rhetoric had nothing to do with the violence. Worse, some national media outlets platformed the terrorists, normalizing the idea that murdering doctors was a principle worthy of debate.

By 1994, the violence and intimidation had gotten so bad that Pres. Clinton signed the FACE (Freedom of Access to Clinic Entrances) Act, making it a federal crime to physically obstruct or use violence or the threat of violence to prevent someone from obtaining reproductive health care services. That year, the Supreme Court ruled that clinics had the right to create "buffer zones" to protect their patients' rights to access."

Despite this, most clinics were left to defend themselves. They hired armed guards, installed bulletproof glass, and took other measures to protect themselves. While the new laws slowed the onslaught, the attacks and killings continued.

***

Back in Arkansas, Huckabee lost his Senate race. But, with Asa Hutchinson's encouragement, he was able to quickly pivot his campaign to the newly opened lieutenant governor's seat in 1993, which he barely won.

So when Huckabee squeaked his way into the lieutenant governor's office, he represented, in fully realized form, the merging of the Evangelical voting bloc with the Republican Party in Arkansas. He even presented himself as the state's "pastor-in-chief." He wrote in his memoir, "There are times when I feel I'm pastoring a 2.5-million-member church."[21] Throughout his memoir, and as a theme running through his entire career, he, like his inspirations James Robison and Jerry Falwell, pushed the idea that more Christians (specifically, Evangelicals) should get involved in politics, to put their God "back" into government. Indeed, he says that it is impossible to separate religion and politics. It's a belief he shares with many on the right, including his old friend Jay Cole. This movement sometimes calls itself "Dominionist," meaning that Christians are meant to "have dominion over" all aspects of society, including government. Another, more accurate, term might be Christian nationalists, though in the mid-1990s, they were still disavowing that label.

***

Though Huckabee frequently, loudly, and publicly insisted that "character" is of the utmost importance in political leaders, that didn't seem to stop him from engaging in a slew of ethically questionable practices while in office. The allegations ran the gamut from just tacky to outright illegal. The most well-known of them was more of an embarrassment than a scandal: in the summer of 2000, the Governor's Mansion, a brick Georgian built in the 1950s, had to undergo some desperately needed renovations, particularly to the plumbing and wiring. So the Huckabees – Mike, Janet, and their three kids – David, John Mark, and future governor herself, Sarah – moved into a manufactured home that had been set up on the grounds of the Governor's Mansion. The home, donated by an Indiana company, was actually quite nice, with over 2,100 square feet of living space. Janet insisted that it was not a trailer: "Trailers are pulled behind a pickup truck," she said. But there was no getting around the simple fact that, for all intents and purposes, it was essentially a triple-wide trailer house. The national media couldn't resist such comedy gold, and the debacle ended up in places like the *New York Times* and Jay Leno's monologue.

But not all his scandals were so innocuous. As lieutenant governor, Huckabee set up a nonprofit to supplement his salary with speaking fees and other perks – to the tune of tens of thousands of dollars – from anonymous donors. He was alleged to have misused the Governor's Mansion expense account for his family's personal living expenses (including groceries and Janet's pantyhose), as well as treating the nearly $70,000 worth of furniture donated to the Governor's Mansion as his to keep.

And, like any good Baptist preacher, he also spent his time in office engaging in "pounding," a common practice in some congregations where they show respect to their pastors by giving them gifts. According to his disclosure reports, Huckabee accepted more than 300 gifts while he was in office, with a total value of at least $130,000. The list of gifts includes $3,700 cowboy boots, a $600 chainsaw, a $500 canoe, and a $200 stadium blanket, just to name a few.[22] Many of his generous benefactors were rewarded with appointments to state commissions or offices, as well as lucrative state contracts. In just one example, Huckabee (with the help of other Republicans in the state legislature) directed millions of dollars in Medicaid funding to an unlicensed, abusive Christian "youth ranch" run by convicted fraudster Ted Suhl (who would later be pardoned by Donald Trump). Over his entire eleven years in office, Huckabee would be the subject of more than two dozen ethics complaints – more than any other Arkansas governor before him, earning the nickname "the Huckster." Despite doing everything in his power to use government to enforce his particular brand of ethics on everyone else, he once told journalist John Brummett that ethics cannot be regulated by government and that procedures set up presuming to do so merely invite harassment by partisan political enemies.[23]

And though he likes to present himself as kindly, soft-spoken, and self-deprecating, he is notoriously petty, vindictive, and thin-skinned. In one instance, when the host of a talk show on Little Rock's PBS affiliate expressed his distaste of Huckabee at a Young Democrats event, Huckabee pressured the station to cancel his show. When called out on it, he publicly claimed he had no knowledge of any effort to cancel the show. Huckabee ended up settling with the host out of court.

But that pales in comparison to how he treated journalist Max Brantley. Brantley began covering Huckabee when he was a columnist for the *Arkansas Gazette*, the state's more progressive paper, and then continued to do so for the *Arkansas Times*, the state's alt weekly. Brantley exposed – and criticized – Huckabee's many ethical violations, and in retaliation, Huckabee compared him to Jeffrey Dahmer. In addition, Max says he was told on good authority that Huckabee "has wished aloud for my early and violent demise."[24] Later, Huckabee would revoke the *Arkansas Times'* press credentials, claiming it wasn't a legitimate newspaper.

Despite all this, Huckabee broke from the GOP platform in some surprisingly progressive ways. He actually *raised* taxes to fund highways and schools, and, after being diagnosed with Type 2 diabetes, made fighting obesity his signature cause, taking on the powerful soft-drink lobby in the process.

He might also be considered "soft on crime" by GOP standards, pardoning or commuting the sentences of more criminals than his three predecessors combined. He apparently did little to no research on these cases before granting pardons and commutations. Instead, he relied on the recommendations of people close to him – mostly Evangelical Christians and pastors like Jay Cole – and the statements of the criminals themselves, especially those who claimed to have "found Jesus." Indeed, Huckabee proudly boasts that he bases his decisions not on facts or logic, but on his faith in God.

Over his ten years in office, Huckabee issued over 1,000 pardons or commutations. And the very first of them was Wayne Dumond.

ENDNOTES:

1. Mike Huckabee with John Perry, *Character IS the Issue: How People with Integrity Can Revolutionize America* (Nashville, Tennessee: Broadman & Holman Publishers, 1997) p. 10.

2. Huckabee and Perry, *Character*.

3. Joe Conason and Gene Lyons, *The Hunting of the Presidency: The Ten-Year Campaign to Destroy Bill and Hillary Clinton* (New York, New York: St. Martin's Press, 2000) p. 249.

4. David Koon, "The Says of our lives," *Arkansas Times*, October 5, 2011.

5. Conason and Lyons, *Hunting of the Presidency*.

6. Aaron Sarlo, "Tucker flips, flops," *Arkansas Times*, July 16, 1996.

7. Mike Huckabee, address to the 5th Annual Meeting of the Conservative Political Action Committee, February 10, 2008.

8. Scott Jester, "A Boyhood Fascination Results in Lifelong Broadcasting Career," HopePrescott.com, May 6, 2022.

9. Huckabee, address.

10. Huckabee and Perry, *Character*, p. 127.

11. Huckabee and Perry, *Character*, p. 139.

12. Huckabee and Perry, *Character*, pp. 47-48.

13. Brian Kaylor, "A 'Transformative Moment' in SBC Political Activity," *Good Faith Media*, August 20, 2010.

14. Huckabee and Perry, *Character*, p. 121.

15. Max Blumenthal, "The Real Mike Huckabee," *The Nation*, January 28, 2008.

16. Huckabee and Perry, *Character*, p. 45.

17. Huckabee and Perry, *Character,* p. 1.

18. Huckabee and Perry, *Character,* pp. 51-53.

19. Max Brantley, "The dark side of Mike Huckabee," Salon.com, November 13, 2007.

20. Huckabee and Perry, *Character,* p. 54.

21. Huckabee and Perry, *Character,* p. 90.

22. Kenneth P. Vogel, "Huckabee rivals unearth ethics complaints," *Politico*, November 21, 2007.

23. John Brummett, "The line between tacky and crooked," *Arkansas Times*, November 15, 2007.

24. Brantley, "Dark side."

Chapter 10: "My Desire is That You be Released From Prison"

After the chaotic events of July 15, 1996, Mike Huckabee was finally in a place to repay his old friend Jay Cole, as well as the (now nationwide) community of fundamentalists and Clinton-haters that had been pushing for Wayne's release for a decade.

Only two months after his swearing-in, Huckabee announced that due to "serious questions as to the legitimacy of his guilt" based on the genetic testing – as well as the fact that Wayne had been castrated, of course – he intended to commute Wayne Dumond's sentence to time served. "In light of the suffering he has already experienced," Huckabee said in a news release, "I am unable to justify his continued incarceration."

This even though the parole board had recently voted – on two separate occasions – not to release Wayne. In late August, they denied him parole, and then in September, only ten days before Huckabee made his announcement, they voted against recommending either executive clemency or pardon.[1]

Arkansas law required Huckabee to wait at least thirty days, but not more than 120, after his announcement to allow the public to give their feedback or objections, meaning that he had to make a final, public decision on releasing Wayne from prison by January 20, 1997.[2]

He was completely unprepared for the public outcry that followed, according to Murray Waas, whose investigative reporting exposed Huckabee's efforts to get Wayne out of prison.

Ashley Stevens, along with twenty women members of the state House of Representatives and several members of law enforcement, staged a protest against Huckabee's decision on the steps of the State Capitol building, sparking renewed media interest in the case.[3]

The elders of Graham Memorial Presbyterian Church wrote to Huckabee – and forwarded their letter to local newspapers – urging him, "Don't Free Dumond." Their letter ends with, "He will hurt someone else's child, Governor, if you let him go. You'll see."[4]

In an effort to stem the political fallout, Waas wrote, Huckabee and his staff agreed to meet with Ashley, her family, and Fletcher Long, the prosecuting attorney who sent Wayne to prison, to hear their side of the story.[5]

Ashley, who was now twenty-nine, tried to persuade Huckabee that Wayne was a dangerous man and should not be set free. But Huckabee had fully bought into the lie that Wayne was innocent, and that Ashley was "mistaken" about who had raped her. So she got right up in Huckabee's face, only inches away from him, and told him, "This is how close I was to Wayne Dumond. I will never forget his face. And now I don't want you ever to forget my face."[6]

Ashley wasn't Wayne's only victim to plead with Huckabee to reconsider freeing Wayne. Waas' investigation turned up letters that Wayne's earlier victims had sent to the governor. The DeWitt woman whom Wayne had raped at knifepoint wrote to him, expressing her guilt: "I feel responsible for Ashley's years of suffering at Dumond's hands because I was so naïve as to believe that since Dumond was arrested for raping me that he had learned his lesson and would not do it again."[7] She also included the police report where Wayne had confessed to raping her, but had refused to sign.

"I feel that if he is released it is only a matter of time before he commits another crime and fear that he will not leave a witness to testify against him the next time," she wrote.[8]

Her daughter, who had only been three years old at the time (and sleeping in the bed next to her) when her mother was attacked, wrote to Huckabee as well, begging him as a fellow Baptist to at least call her and talk to her. He never did.[9]

Despite all this, Waas wrote that the Stevenses and Long came away from that meeting frustrated that Huckabee seemed to know so little about the case. Waas quotes Long: "He [Huckabee] kept insisting that there was DNA evidence that has since exonerated Dumond, when that very much wasn't the case. No matter that that wasn't true … we couldn't seem to say or do anything to disabuse him of that notion."[10]

Waas also quotes an anonymous state official who advised Huckabee on the case: "I don't believe that he had access to, or read, the law enforcement records or parole commission's files — even by then," the official said. "He already seemed to have made up his mind, and his knowledge of the case appeared to be limited to a large degree as to what people had told him, what Jay Cole had told him, and what he had read in the *New York Post*."[11]

Indeed, in the decade since his conviction, Wayne's cause had moved from the editorial pages and AM talk shows in Arkansas into the national anti-Clinton media. Primed by a decade of the broader right-wing media's constant stream of conspiracy theories and allegations against the Clintons (which never managed to turn up anything of substance), many people were willing to believe that the Clintons were capable of anything. As Amanda Marcotte put it, "By the late '90s, it was an all-out Roman feast of paranoid bullshit for Clinton haters."[12] It wasn't hard to convince them that Wayne was an innocent man who had been castrated and falsely imprisoned by the "Clinton machine."

Steve Dunleavy, a correspondent for Rupert Murdoch-owned tabloid TV show *A Current Affair*, then later, a columnist for another Murdoch-owned tabloid, the *New York Post*, had also taken up Wayne's cause. His columns pushed easily verifiable lies, like that Wayne had no criminal record and that DNA evidence had exonerated him. Worse, he frequently referred to Ashley as a "so-called victim" and flat out wrote, "That rape never happened."[13]

Thanks to Waas' investigation, we now know that on October 31, 1996 – after the protests, the letters from Wayne's victims, and the meeting with Ashley – Huckabee met with the parole board. What actually happened at that meeting is unclear; Huckabee's version of events is at odds with that of several board members who later spoke out about it. The minutes of that meeting only state: "Governor Mike Huckabee and the board went into executive session. The board appreciates the governor meeting with them to discuss his and other concerns regarding criminal justice and rehabilitation and sharing his viewpoints on other issues."[14]

One of the board members told Waas that at the meeting, which Huckabee had called, he said to them, "There is this one case I want to talk to you about."[15]

It was at that point, according to Waas' reporting, that the chair of the board, Leroy Brownlee, had the meeting go into a closed-door executive session. This seems to have been a violation of Arkansas' Freedom of Information Act, which says state boards may only meet privately for the "specific purpose of considering employment, appointment, promotion, demotion, disciplining or resignation of any public officer or employee."[16]

At least four board members questioned the propriety of the board going into a closed-door session to discuss a specific case. "The board is supposed to be autonomous," one board member told Waas. "Whenever we all come together, the public is supposed to be notified by law. And we should have never been in executive session with a governor about anything."[17]

Another board member told Waas, "Some of us were taken aback when the chairman took us into executive session. ... He should have known better than to do that, and presumably most of us knew better as well ... you can't do that. The only reason a state board can ever go into executive session is to discuss personnel matters."[18]

"And so when the press called and wanted to know why Mr. Brownlee wanted to go into executive session, we said we didn't know why," a board member said. "We couldn't answer that question. What were we going to say? That he was protecting the governor? That's exactly what it was. The governor started talking about Dumond, so Mr. Brownlee knew that was inappropriate, and he went into executive session in order to allow the governor to speak without the press being there."[19]

A Huckabee spokesperson later admitted that the meeting might have in fact violated FOIA laws, but that it was Brownlee's decision to go into executive session, and the governor wasn't familiar enough with the statute to object.[20]

Despite the fact that the meeting was closed, there still should have been a record of it, according to board members and staff. They told Waas that the board's office administrator ordinarily attended the meetings and took notes. However, they say that at this meeting, Brownlee asked her to leave the room when the board went into executive session. A spokesman for the board told Waas that there is no record of what occurred in that meeting — no tape recording, notes, or minutes.[21]

When asked, Huckabee denied that he supported Dumond's parole during that part of the meeting, but several of the board members told a very different story. They say that Huckabee made it clear that he favored a commutation of Dumond's sentence.[22]

"The governor felt strongly that Dumond had gotten a raw deal," according to one board member. "He said the sentence was awfully excessive for what he did. I said, 'Governor, well that happens. When you rape a cheerleader in a small town like that, that's what is going to happen.'

"He responded, 'Most people don't get a life sentence plus twenty years.'

"I pointed out that his sentence had already been reduced to thirty-nine and a half years and said, 'That's not really out of line at all.'"[23]

The board member said that most of the other members remained silent as he and Huckabee argued over the issue. "I got the impression that no one wanted to argue with the governor," he said.[24] Indeed, seats on the parole board – officially, the Post Prison Transfer Board – are political patronage jobs. Members are appointed, or re-appointed, to their positions by the governor.

Following that meeting, again according to Waas' reporting, Brownlee then took a series of highly unusual steps to help Wayne gain his freedom.

On November 29, 1996, Dumond sent a request for reconsideration of his bid for parole to the board. Ordinarily, inmates have to wait a full year from their last hearing to go before the board again. In Dumond's case, his next hearing would have been scheduled for August 29, 1997.[25]

For an inmate to obtain a new board hearing under such circumstances, Waas writes, only one board member needs to approve his request. So, if the request is approved by the first board member who reads it, the hearing is then scheduled, and no further vote is needed. Brownlee was the first person to read his request and approve it, so no other board members were given a copy of his request to review.[26]

In fact, no copy of that request, or Brownlee's approval, exists. The board told Waas that it's likely the document had been misplaced, "if it ever existed."[27]

Nevertheless, Brownlee's approval granted Wayne a new parole hearing. But there was a wrinkle: as long as Wayne was in Cummins, he couldn't be scheduled for a new hearing before January 20, 1997, which was Huckabee's deadline to act on his announcement that he was considering commuting Dumond's sentence.[28]

So, immediately after approving Wayne's request for a hearing, from December 1996 to January 1997, Brownlee was in regular contact with Butch Reeves, Huckabee's prison liaison, according to two state officials. During those discussions, Brownlee expressed frustration that the hearing was likely to be delayed because Dumond was incarcerated at Cummins.[29]

That month – December – Wayne was transferred from Cummins to the Tucker unit. His sudden transfer was explained in conflicting ways — one prison official said it was because the warden wanted to break up a "clique" that Wayne was a part of, another said it was out of concern for his safety, and another said it was a routine transfer so that he could get a different prison job.

Regardless, this transfer allowed him to get on the Tucker unit's parole hearing schedule, which would allow the board to parole him before Huckabee's deadline — thus taking the heat for his release off Huckabee.[30]

On January 9, 1997, in a rare move, Brownlee personally interviewed Wayne at Tucker. Following that interview, Brownlee recommended to the full board that he be paroled, on the condition that he leave the state of Arkansas.[31]

One week later – and four days before Huckabee's deadline – on January 16, 1997, the Post Prison Transfer Board voted four to one, with two abstentions, to grant Wayne Dumond parole on the condition that he leave Arkansas.

That day, Huckabee released a public statement: "I concur with the board's action and hope the lives of all those involved can move forward. The action of the board accomplishes what I sought to do in considering an earlier request for commutation …

"In light of the action of the board, my original intent to commute the sentence to time served is no longer relevant."[32]

He then wrote to Wayne personally: "Dear Wayne, I have reviewed your applications for executive clemency, specifically a commutation and/or pardon. … My desire is that you be released from prison. I feel now that parole is the best way for your reintegration into society. … Therefore, after careful consideration … I have denied your applications."

Wayne would be freed, and Huckabee could wash his hands of the whole affair – at least, for a while.

Wayne wasn't just going to walk out the front door of the prison immediately, though. There were various bureaucratic and administrative obstacles to overcome – the biggest of which would be finding a state willing to let Wayne move to, since he wouldn't be able to live in Arkansas. Dusty had originally planned to have Wayne come live with her and her family in Houston, but the State of Texas refused to admit him. So did Missouri and Florida.

So Wayne would remain in prison for almost two more years after the parole board's decision to free him.

ENDNOTES:

1. Murray S. Waas, "Web special: Dumond case revisited," *Arkansas Times*, 2002, updated September 1, 2005.

2. Waas, "Web special."

3. Waas, "Web special."

4. "Don't Free Dumond," Clipping from unmarked newspaper, Jack Hill papers, Special Collections, Series 3, Box 42, Folder 16.

5. Waas, "Web special."

6. Murray S. Waas, "Documents Expose Huckabee's Role in Serial Rapist's Release," *Huffington Post*, March 28, 2008.

7. Waas, "Documents expose Huckabee's."

8. Waas, "Documents expose Huckabee's."

9. Waas, "Documents expose Huckabee's."

10. Waas, "Web special."

11. Waas, "Web special."

12. Amanda Marcotte, "The Clinton BS Files: "Lock her up" isn't really about emails — the right's been accusing the Clintons of murder for decades," Salon.com, August 29, 2016.

13. Steve Dunleavy, "Clinton's Biggest Crime: Left Innocent Man in Jail for 14 Years," *New York Post*, September 21, 1999.

14. Waas, "Web special."

15. Waas, "Web special."

16. Waas, "Web special."

17. Waas, "Web special."

18. Waas, "Web special."

19. Waas, "Web special."

20. Waas, "Web special."

21. Waas, "Web special."

22. Waas, "Web special."

23. Waas, "Web special."

24. Waas, "Web special."

25. Waas, "Web special."

26. Waas, "Web special."

27. Waas, "Web special."

28. Waas, "Web special."

29. Waas, "Web special."

30. Waas, "Web special."

31. Waas, "Web special."

32. Waas, "Web special."

PART II

Chapter 11: Missouri

When Wayne Dumond finally walked out of the Tucker unit in late September 1999, he had, somehow, been able to bypass the parole board's condition that he had to leave the state, because he was allowed to move back to DeWitt and live with his dad and stepmom.

His family was ecstatic that their long battle was won, and Wayne was finally going to be free. Bobby, his younger brother, had been saving up the catfish he caught out of the Arkansas River, and he hosted a big fish fry for his whole family when Wayne got out. Wayne was even offered a job as a welder at the family business.[1]

Former neighbors and classmates in DeWitt were less enthusiastic, though. One woman, the wife of the pastor at the church Wayne and Dusty had attended, said people in town were "fearful, reluctant" and "uneasy" and that some were obliquely – or outright – threatening to kill him. Even the mayor said, "More than one person has expressed an interest in doing Mr. Dumond bodily harm, up to and including the termination of his life."[2]

His family waved the concerns away as "people not knowing the whole story." And indeed, some in DeWitt believed the conspiracy theories. "If it had been anybody else besides Clinton's cousin, I don't think he'd have got the conviction he got," one woman told News at 6.[3]

But the one person who had worked the hardest for his release, and who had been yearning for it more than anyone, wasn't there.

Back in January, Dusty had been in Columbus, Ohio, visiting relatives for the holidays, when she was involved in a car wreck. She suffered fatal injuries and died on January 8, 1999.

It didn't take Wayne too long, though, to find himself another older, church-going woman. Terry Sue Wood had been part of a church group from the Kansas City area that had taken on Wayne's cause, and she had traveled to Arkansas with them to visit him in prison. At some point, they fell in love – or at least Terry Sue did – and so in early August of 2000, the two were married in her hometown of Smithville, Missouri, a small suburb of Kansas City.

Now that he had a documented connection to Missouri, he re-applied to the state to have his parole moved there, and this time, it was approved. He had to register as a sex offender and, according to reporting from the Memphis *Commercial Appeal*, meet on a weekly basis with a parole officer who specialized in sex offenders. He was also enrolled in a private sex offender treatment program, though the name and nature of that program isn't reported[4] (I only mention it because in this part of the country, many "treatment programs" are not, in fact, licensed addiction or mental healthcare providers, but rather, unlicensed "Biblically based" programs staffed by unqualified "counselors," and are nothing more than well financed Bible study classes).

Wayne was able to get a job with a furniture factory in nearby Edgerton doing what he'd done back in Forrest City: cabinetmaking. It was a job that was in high demand, since the north part of Kansas City was experiencing a boom in the construction of new apartment buildings and houses.

Six weeks after Wayne and Terry Sue's wedding, early on the morning of September 20, Wayne briefly met with his parole officer, Robert Trotter, and said he felt like he had a stomach virus and wouldn't be able to make it to work that day.

When Terry Sue came home from work that evening, she found Wayne passed out on the garage floor, an empty bottle of Jack Daniels next to him. He had scratches on his face, a swollen shoulder and elbow, and a bruise on his thigh. He told her he'd gotten them from falling down some stairs.

The next day, he went to see a doctor for his injuries. The day after that, Wayne called Trotter again and told him that he had hurt his shoulder and back falling down some stairs. The next time they met, about a week later, Trotter said he could see scratches and bruises on Wayne's face, which he again attributed to that fall down the stairs.

Around the same time Terry Sue was arriving home to find Wayne passed out on the garage floor, Rick Matthews and his roommate came home from work to find their Kansas City North apartment in shambles. Furniture and pictures were strewn around and broken; something violent had clearly happened there.

When, following the trail of destruction, Matthews made his way back to his bedroom, he discovered that this was something far worse than a robbery. His girlfriend, Carol, was lying on the bed, her nude body partially covered with a towel, a ripped plastic bag lying next to her. Panicked, he tried to call 911, but the phone cord had been ripped from the wall.

In processing the scene, investigators were able to determine that Matthews' girlfriend, Carol Sue Shields, had been in the apartment that morning – her keys were on the kitchen table, along with a note she had written to his roommate.

Carol, a thirty-nine-year-old mother and hotel sales manager, was married, but was having an affair with Matthews and spending a lot of time at his apartment.

In questioning neighbors, investigators learned that they had heard her screaming, as well as a lot of "thumping around," at about nine that morning, which would have been minutes after Carol had arrived at the apartment and written the note.

She had apparently fought her attacker, and the fight had taken place throughout several rooms of the apartment. During the struggle, her attacker pulled out a clump of her hair, and she was left with injuries and bruises on her head, face, elbows, hands, legs, and foot.

At some point during the attack, she had managed to get the phone and dial 911, but the call was disconnected – probably by her attacker ripping the cord out of the wall – before she could say anything. Police officers had been dispatched to the apartment sometime later, but left after getting no response from inside the apartment or from neighbors.

In the end, her attacker was able to subdue her and bind her wrists and ankles, likely with zip ties. He then removed all her clothes and cut off her bra before sexually assaulting her.

Finally, he put a plastic bag over her head, asphyxiating her.

Before he left, he cleaned up the crime scene. He removed the zip ties from her ankles and wrists and took them with him, along with all her clothes. He also took the time to wipe away all his fingerprints before he left.

Fortunately, her attacker hadn't cleaned up everything. A small piece of her bra was found under her body, and several of his hairs had been left on the bed. She also had some of his skin under her fingernails. The hairs and skin were collected and sent for DNA analysis, which would likely take months.

The investigators' first suspects were, naturally, her husband and her boyfriend. But they didn't have anything tying either of them to the crime, and until the DNA results came back, her killer would remain at large.

***

Since his release, the right-wing fervor on Wayne's behalf had faded; after all, they got what they wanted. But he was still one of their poster boys, a "victim" of the Clintons' machinations. So in early March 2001, about six months after Carol Sue Shields' murder, Ward Harkavy of *The Village Voice* dragged Wayne back into the spotlight to get his thoughts on the controversial Marc Rich pardon.

On his last day in office, Bill Clinton had pardoned Rich, who was convicted of tax fraud, racketeering, and engaging in illegal oil deals with Iran. Notably, James Comey had been the prosecutor in that case.[5] Both Democrats and Republicans had criticized the pardon and launched an investigation to determine if it had been illegally "bought" by Rich's wife via her hefty donations to the DNC, the Clinton Presidential Library, and Hillary's New York senate campaign.

In his column "The Castration of Wayne Dumond," Harkavy rehashes the old claim that Stevie Stevens was "part of a Democratic machine that ruled the Arkansas Delta and nurtured Clinton's career," and that Coolidge Conlee was a Clinton "ally," along with the other standard lies about the case, like that there was no evidence linking Wayne to the crime.

Harkavy describes Wayne as "chuckling" and "laughing" during the interview, presumably at the irony that Clinton is so corrupt that he (allegedly) would sell a pardon to a billionaire crony like Rich, while simultaneously keeping a poor, innocent man like Wayne behind bars. But maybe Wayne had something else to laugh about.

***

Three more months rolled by, and Carol's murder case was still in limbo. The DNA from the skin found under her fingernails was processed, and it showed that it had come from only two donors: Carol herself and an unknown male donor. Carol's husband, Matthews, and Matthews' roommate were all excluded as possible donors.

The unknown DNA profile was entered into the national database to try and find a match. On June 21, 2001, investigators in Clay County were still waiting on the Arkansas Crime Lab to send them the identity of that unknown donor.

On June 21, 2001, Sara Andrasek was twenty-three and living with her husband in an apartment in Kansas City North. She had graduated summa cum laude from Kansas' Ottawa University the previous year with a bachelor's degree in sociology.[6] And they had only recently discovered that Sara was pregnant with their first child.

On June 21, 2001, Wayne was working on Northridge Road, less than 10 minutes away from the Andraseks' apartment. At about 1 p.m., he left the job site.[7] Sara's husband had left Sara alone in the apartment only an hour earlier.

When he came home later that afternoon, he found Sara's body, naked, on the bed, which had been stripped of its sheets. Other clues indicated that her killer had cleaned up the scene before he left – though he missed one small thing: a tiny piece of rope that had lodged in the bathtub drain.

Later evidence would show that she had been sexually assaulted and strangled to death.

And though the two murders had happened in two different counties – Carol's was in Clay County, and Sara's was in Platte County – the similarities between the two were too obvious to ignore.

The very next day, June 22, the results from the DNA test finally came back from Arkansas: it was a match for Wayne Dumond.

Since Wayne was still on parole, he was easy to find. Within hours of receiving the DNA results, officers arrested Wayne on parole violations. They searched his home and his workplace, where they found a plastic zip tie similar to the ones used on Carol, as well as rope similar to that found at Sara's crime scene. Police also seized computer equipment, latex gloves, paycheck stubs, and canceled checks.

They also took a hair sample from him, which would later be a match with the hairs found on the bed, based on mitochondrial DNA.

Wayne was charged with first-degree murder. He pled not guilty, but since he was still on parole, he was denied bail. He would have to sit in prison while he waited for his day in court.

Wayne's trial for the murder of Carol Sue Shields began in early November of 2003. This trial was very different than his first one; while there were certainly reporters covering it, it was nowhere near as big of a story as his first trial. There weren't crowds of people waiting to get into the courtroom, either, though Terry Sue was there, as was Carol's mother, Lois Davidson.

Notably, the pundits, pastors, talk show hosts, and politicians who had championed Wayne's cause were nowhere to be found. The right-wing media ecosphere was completely silent.

Wayne's attorney filed for a change of venue, claiming he couldn't get a fair trial in Clay County. So, rather than move the trial, the court agreed to choose jurors from Nodaway County and have them transported in.

The trial was fairly straightforward: Wayne had no alibi for the time of the murder, and the DNA evidence from the tissue under Carol's fingernails, as well as from hairs found on the bed, placed him at the crime scene. The scratches and bruises he received on the day of her murder corroborated the evidence against him. There was also supporting evidence found at his workplace, like the zip tie and pieces of Carol's bra.

His defense did the best it could, trying to throw doubt on the DNA evidence and pointing the finger at Carol's husband, claiming he was abusive. But it didn't work. After deliberating for three hours, the jury found him guilty. The following summer, he was sentenced to life in prison without the possibility of parole.

***

Meanwhile, newly elected Platte County Prosecutor Eric Zahnd had taken on Sara Andrasek's case – his very first since taking office. He patiently continued building a case against Wayne for Sara's murder. They had found genetic material in a latex glove found at Wayne's workplace that had Sara's DNA on it, and the rope found there was nearly identical to the kind found in Sara's bathtub drain.

But with Wayne now permanently behind bars, it didn't seem like there was any need for urgency. In 2005, Zahnd was getting ready to bring capital murder charges against

Wayne, intending to seek the death penalty. But, in a bit of poetic justice, Wayne beat him to it. Wayne, who had used his voice to lie and deceive so much, developed cancer of the vocal cords.

On August 31, 2005, he was found dead in his cell at the Crossroads Correctional Center in Cameron, Missouri.

ENDNOTES:

1. "Parole of Rapist Stirs Resentment, Fear in Hometown." News at 6, September 27, 1999.

2. "Parole of Rapist."

3. "Parole of Rapist."

4. Bartholomew Sullivan, "Dumond Linked to Missouri Slaying; Kansas City Cops Search Home, Worksite," *The Commercial Appeal*, June 26, 2001.

5. Jessica Taylor, "More Surprises: FBI Releases Files On Bill Clinton's Pardon Of Marc Rich," NPR.org, November 1, 2016.

6. Benita Williams, "Police attempt to link killings – Northland women died similarly," *The Kansas City Star*, June 29, 2001, p. B1.

7. Williams, "Police attempt."

PART III

Chapter 12: The 2008 Primaries and Citizens United

"My name is Lois Davidson." An elderly woman, her wavy silver hair cut short and close to her head, looks into the camera, her blue eyes distorted behind wire-rimmed glasses. "My daughter was raped and murdered by Wayne Dumond."

As she holds a picture frame containing a photo of Carol, along with her funeral program, a deep, authoritative male voice similar to Bill Kurtis' intones: "Carol Sue Shields was brutally murdered by Wayne Dumond." Cut to Wayne's mug shot. "Dumond was in an Arkansas prison for raping a seventeen-year-old high-school cheerleader," he continues, as an image of Mike Huckabee appears next to Wayne's. "Until Governor Mike Huckabee helped him get out."

The voiceover briefly goes into how Huckabee helped Wayne get out, and how Wayne raped and murdered Carol. Text from Huckabee's letter to Wayne stating, "My desire is that you be released from prison" fills the screen.

Then Lois Davidson comes back on. "If not for Mike Huckabee, Wayne Dumond would've been in prison, and Carol Sue would be with us," she says, giving the final word in this less-than-one-minute ad.

The final image is of text stating, "Paid for by Victims Voice and not authorized by any candidate, campaign, or committee."[1]

The ad, as well as the non-profit Victims Voice, was created by an Arkansas-based Democratic media consultant named Keith Emis. The ad, which he insists was not paid for by any candidate of any party, was uploaded to YouTube in January 2008, when then-presidential primary candidate Mike Huckabee was gaining in the polls.

In January 2007, Huckabee was facing the end of his time in office. Yet again, he stood in Clinton's shadow: Huckabee had served for a full decade, but would end up two years shy of Clinton's twelve years, thanks to Arkansas' new gubernatorial term limits.

So Huckabee formed an exploratory committee to scope out the prospects for a presidential run. And, in keeping with his habit of playing fast and loose with the rules, just on the heels of launching that committee, he ordered the destruction of nearly 100 computer hard drives and servers taken from the state Capitol building; a state office in Washington, D.C.; the Arkansas State Police airport hangar; the governor's mansion; and – weirdly – the Arkansas State Police drug office. He used $13,000 of the state's emergency fund to destroy them, and the incoming Democratic governor, Mike Beebe, would have to spend $335,000 to replace them.[2]

The director of the state's Department of Information Systems said that her office had backed up the information from the servers, but not the hard drives. The office had given those backup tapes to Huckabee's former chief of staff, and had not kept any copies.[3]

Democratic state Sen. Jimmy Jeffress told *Computerworld* magazine that he was shocked at the lengths Huckabee had gone to to destroy records. "This is typical for what we've experienced the last ten years out of Mr. Huckabee," he said. "It sort of reminds me a lot of what [President Richard] Nixon did before he left office — trying to erase tapes."[4]

Huckabee defended his actions, stating that he did so "to protect sensitive information, such as employees' or constituents' Social Security numbers and credit card information." The state's attorney general would later clear Huckabee of any wrongdoing.

Before the end of the month, on January 28, 2007, Huckabee went on *Meet the Press* to officially announce his candidacy for president. And though he impressed many pundits on both sides with his down-to-earth, affable charm, he was still a dark-horse candidate in a crowded race. He didn't have any name recognition outside of his home state, and he wasn't pulling in the big donors like his rivals Mitt Romney and John McCain.

But say what you will about the man, he is smart and knows how to politic. On a shoestring budget, using mostly volunteers (including his daughter, Sarah), he worked to get himself in front of as many voters as possible. His volunteer staff, which he called "Huck's Army," included several younger, tech-savvy folks who set him up with social media profiles on Myspace, Facebook, and YouTube. He called this his "secret weapon," and it did translate into quite a bit of support from younger voters.

He was there on the opening day of pheasant season in Iowa, showing off his bona fides as a game bird hunter, and he played his bass guitar at several of his stump events in that state, both as a soloist and with his band, Capitol Offense.

Once again, mirroring Clinton's campaign, he appeared on all the late-night comedy shows, including the staunchly left-leaning *The Colbert Report* and *The Daily Show With Jon Stewart*.

Indeed, campaigning on television was when he was in his element, considering all his years spent in front of the camera as a minister. He was quick on the uptake, able to answer serious questions in detail, but also able to think on his feet and come back with snappy zingers.

While his platform mostly consisted of the standard GOP planks of strong national defense, lower taxes, outlawing abortion and gay marriage, defending the rights of gun owners, and slashing social programs, he broke from his GOP rivals by acknowledging climate change and speaking out against big money interests. While he could never articulate how exactly he intended to rein in corporate greed – he was adamant that government regulation was not the answer – he did at least seem to understand that it was a problem that needed to be solved.

His Reagan-like charisma and populist messaging won over a lot of moderate Republicans. And he set himself apart from the pack by reaching out to African Americans, as well, speaking at events at Morgan State University and the Urban League in St. Louis.

But his biggest base was, of course, the Evangelicals. At the Values Voters Debate in Fort Lauderdale, he won the post-debate straw poll by sixty percent, in what he calls a "blowout."[5] He was endorsed by such big names in the right as Jerry Falwell, Jr.; James Dobson; and (belatedly) Paul Weyrich, along with at least a dozen other Evangelical leaders.

In January 2008, he won the Iowa caucuses, giving him a surprise lead in the crowded (and much better funded) field of candidates. The more people saw of him, the more they liked him, and he climbed steadily in the polls. On Super Tuesday, he won five states: West Virginia, Georgia, Alabama, Tennessee, and his home state of Arkansas. He went on to win Kansas and in Louisiana (though because he hadn't earned fifty percent of the vote, he wasn't awarded any delegates).

But despite his modest success in his charm offensive, the story of the Dumond Affair had broken into the national media.

As early as 2006, the *Arkansas Times* and other Arkansas media outlets had been trying to get access to the records of the parole board's meeting with Huckabee, but were getting stonewalled – or attacked – by the governor's office. The *Arkansas Times*, which had long been critical of Huckabee, was far out in front of the others in investigating the Dumond Affair. For that, in May of 2006, Huckabee's office had rescinded the *Times'* press credentials.

But now, with Huckabee running for president, reporter Murray Waas broke the full story of Huckabee's role in getting Wayne released – as well as how he had attempted to cover it up – in the *Arkansas Times*.

Quoting a former Huckabee staffer, Waas wrote that during Huckabee's 2002 gubernatorial re-election bid, Huckabee attended a meeting where he and his top aides expressed concerns that information in Dumond's files – i.e., the letters Wayne's victims sent to Huckabee – might somehow become public. Another senior aide suggested asking other state agencies that might have portions of Wayne's file to transfer their records to Huckabee's office. The reasoning was, if all the files were transferred to the governor's office, they could be classified as "working papers," and no longer covered by the state's Freedom of Information Act.

So the information stayed hidden, and Huckabee won re-election.

When Wayne was arrested for Carol Sue Shields' murder, the media spotlight had been thrown onto Huckabee – but outside of Missouri and Arkansas, it didn't amount to much. When Huckabee was questioned about it, he would claim he had no part in getting Wayne released. And the right-wing media that had clamored so loudly for Wayne's release were silent. Never did any of the writers or pundits come out and apologize or admit they were wrong. Instead, the Dumond Affair was simply tossed down the memory hole.

But now, with Huckabee stepping out onto the national stage, the Dumond Affair followed him. The bombshell information in the Emis video first went public in November of 2007, and soon afterwards, the national media took up the story. In early December, CBS' *Early Show*, ABC's *Good Morning America*, and MSNBC's *Morning Joe,* all covered it, including doing interviews with Lois Davidson.

CNN's Wolf Blitzer had Huckabee on via video to answer questions about it on December 7. When Blitzer asks him if he bore any responsibility for the tragedy, Huckabee weasels around it: "My only official action in this is I denied his commutation." He then quickly pivots to blaming Jim Guy Tucker (who did, in fact, commute Wayne's sentence) and Bill Clinton. Huckabee says that Wayne met the criteria for parole and he supported it, "but I didn't parole Dumond."[6] Indeed, all the behind-the-scenes maneuvering by Leroy Brownlee had been undertaken specifically so Huckabee could say all of this and not technically be lying.

Blitzer then quotes Huckabee's letter to Wayne back to him, emphasizing the line, "My desire is for you to be released from prison." Huckabee sidesteps, saying that that letter was written to notify Wayne that he, Huckabee, would not be granting him a commutation.[7] Again, he didn't technically lie. But left unsaid was that the reason he denied Wayne a commutation was that the board had granted him parole instead.

Then Blitzer asks him about the reporting from the *Arkansas Times*, quoting Waas' article revealing how Huckabee had pushed for Wayne's parole. And that's when Huckabee, the pastor and champion of "character," lies his ass off.

Huckabee claims he was invited to that parole board meeting – which was not true; several board members stated that he called the meeting. He then claims that Wayne's case "just came up." Again, a lie. And then he says that the meeting wasn't about Wayne Dumond specifically, but "my general policy toward clemency."[8]

He then notes his accusers were all appointed by previous, Democratic, governors (and makes sure to name-check Bill Clinton again), and that the ones who spoke out were all members who he had declined to re-appoint to their positions (implying they were disgruntled). He then acts disgusted that people were "politicizing" the tragedy.[9]

The early December media blitz about the Dumond Affair wasn't the end of it, though. In January 2008, when the real primary voting started, Emis bought commercial time for the ad to air on South Carolina television stations during the Republican primary debates in Myrtle Beach. Waas updated his original *Arkansas Times* article for the *Huffington Post*, complete with links to the letters from Wayne's victims, and it was published that March.

The Romney campaign even shot a similar ad featuring Sara Andrasek's mother, Janet Williams, instead. But the ad never aired; Romney decided that airing such a negative ad against someone who wasn't even the front-runner would seem "desperate."[10]

Lois and Janet repeatedly criticized Huckabee not only for letting Dumond go free, but for never apologizing or admitting he was wrong. They say no one from Arkansas, except Ashley Stevens, ever called them.

In every interview where Huckabee is asked about the Dumond Affair, he does the same song and dance: he denies that he had anything to do with Wayne's release (despite what the parole board members have said), claims "no one could have known" that he would commit any more crimes (despite Wayne's victims specifically warning him of that very thing), and then accuses his critics of politicizing the issue (despite how Wayne's cause was taken up specifically as a political issue to attack Bill Clinton).

While the Dumond Affair might not have been the fatal blow to Huckabee's candidacy – he was still far behind the GOP's frontrunner, John McCain – it certainly didn't help. In March 2008, after losing the Texas primary to McCain, Huckabee dropped out of the race.

But that wasn't the end of Huckabee's career. In June, Fox News – the unofficial landing pad for failed Republican politicians – brought him on as a political commentator and contributor to their 2008 presidential election coverage. By that fall, he was back where he was happiest: television, when Fox gave him his own eponymous weekend show. ABC Networks (now Cumulus Media Networks) also got him back into his first love, radio, by signing him to a daily talk-radio show called *The Huckabee Report*.

***

The screen opens with white text floating on a black background, the font reminiscent of an old-school typewriter. It reads: "The problem with nostalgia is what we tend to do is only remember what you like and you forget the parts you didn't." – John Edwards.[11]

The quote moves slowly toward the viewer while a deep, ominous sound, like something underwater, plays. Then high-pitched strings play a drawn-out, creepy note, the soundtrack of a horror movie.

The string music continues into a fast-paced classical-sounding piece while images of headlines frantically flip onto the screen, too quickly to read. If you pause, you can see that they are all about Hillary Clinton, the accusations against her, questions about her testimony, and the like.

Occasionally, the camera zooms in on words like "perjury," "lies," and "veracity." One all-caps, tabloid headline, "Hillary's Web of Deception," lingers on screen longer than the rest.

Then the screen fills with a tight shot of Hillary's face, the kind of candid shot where she's not speaking or smiling, just looking slightly off to her right. Then another picture of her comes on screen, one where she's at a lectern speaking, pointing her finger for emphasis.

The first words are finally spoken by an unidentified woman (it's Angela "Bay" Buchanan, right-wing pundit and Pat Buchanan's sister): "She's driven by the power. She's driven to get the power. That is the driving force in her life."[12]

Next, an unidentified man (Bob Novak, another conservative pundit) proclaims to the camera that "she doesn't answer questions, straight out." Then another woman, again unidentified (but it's Ann Coulter), proceeds to tell the viewer that "she is the expert in not saying what she believes."[13]

And that is how the "documentary," *Hillary: The Movie*, continues for another hour and twenty minutes. The rest of the video is one conservative talking head after another – besides Buchanan, Novak, and Coulter, Newt Gingrich makes an appearance, as do Larry Kudlow, Dick Morris, Michael Medved, and Bill Clinton's accuser, Kathleen Willey, though most of them are never identified. R. Emmett Tyrell of the Arkansas Project narrates parts of the film.

Besides a few clips of Hillary's voice – her benign campaign announcement and a few clips from her speeches, either slowed down to sound ominous or sped up to sound shrill – the whole film consists of a bunch of Republicans (and a couple disgruntled former employees) smearing her character. The talking heads – none of whom actually knew or worked with the Clintons – call her ruthless, power-mad, vindictive, intolerant, and more. Coulter calls her a liar and a psychopath. They harp on how she and her husband were "mired in scandal" – as though the years of right-wing smears and allegations were evidence of her wrongdoing. The whole film is like if Gingrich's "Language: A Key Mechanism of Control" memo had been made into a video.

Hillary: The Movie was created by an organization called Citizens United, which was founded in 1988 by Floyd Brown and David Bossie, both major players in the Arkansas Project/Whitewater scandal. Brown was a former staffer for Bob Dole who "specialized in smearing liberal political figures" and, when Bill Clinton was running in 1992, had launched a newsletter called *ClintonWatch*, which was designed to warn Americans against Clinton's "radical socialist agenda."[14] David Brock quotes one of Brown's screeds, where he summons up the two biggest boogeymen to the right: "Bill Clinton's America sees no difference between families of 'homosexual lovers,' and the traditional, monogamous, faithful family. In addition, Mr. Clinton has completely surrendered to the pro-abortion feminists who dominate the Democratic Party."[15]

Bossie, Citizens United's co-founder and president until 2016, had been Brown's point man on Whitewater, acting as a direct pipeline from the loonies in the Arkansas Project to Republicans in Congress, and was in regular contact with other Arkansas Project players like Jim Johnson, Parker Dozhier, and David Hale.[16] He was also close with Newt Gingrich and Dan Burton, the leader of the anti-Clinton investigations in the House.[17] Those connections got Bossie appointed as chief investigator for the House of Representatives' Committee on Government Reform and Oversight, where he focused on translating Republican attacks against the Clintons into ostensibly legitimate Congressional investigations.

Citizens United's funding appears to come from two main sources: the Koch Brothers (or now, just the Koch family) and its own LLC, The Presidential Coalition, a political action committee also headed by Bossie.

Its work to elect Republicans (and take down Democrats) through producing blatantly one-sided "documentaries" was a brainchild of Bossie's. "I took my motivation one hundred percent from Michael Moore" and Moore's anti-Bush documentary *Fahrenheit 9/11*, Bossie told *The Washington Post*.[18]

He recalled in that interview that Citizens United turned the basement of its offices – housed in a converted townhouse on Pennsylvania Avenue – into a production studio.[19]

From there it went on to produce over two dozen films, including *The Truth Revealed...Confidential Report: Bill Clinton, Al Gore, and the Communist Chinese Connection* (1999); *ACLU: At War With America* (2006); and *Finding God in America*, released the same year as *Hillary: The Movie*, 2008. Its most recent project is *Trump's Rescue Mission: Saving America*, released in late September 2024, which can be watched on their website – for $9.99 – or purchased on DVD for $14.99 plus $5 shipping and handling.

From the minute Hillary announced she was forming an exploratory committee to consider running for president in late January 2007, Citizens United – or rather, its PAC, The Presidential Coalition – leapt into action. Bob Novak and Dick Morris sent out emails under The Presidential Coalition's banner soliciting funds specifically to make a documentary critical of her.

That film – *Hillary: The Movie* – was originally scheduled to be offered as video-on-demand on cable television right before the Democratic primaries a year later, in January 2008. But it ran into a problem: the Federal Election

Commission, rightfully, categorized it as "electioneering" and, under McCain-Feingold campaign finance laws, barred it from advertising or paying to have it broadcast on cable TV. It could still be released in theaters and sold on DVD, though.[20]

Citizens United appealed to a Washington, D.C., federal court and lost. That court, made up of a panel of judges, upheld the FEC's decision, stating "the film was a ninety-minute campaign ad ... susceptible of no other interpretation than to inform the electorate that Senator Clinton is unfit for office, that the United States would be a dangerous place in a President Hillary Clinton world, and that viewers should vote against her."[21]

So Citizens United appealed that decision to the Supreme Court. Unfortunately for Citizens United, that hearing wouldn't take place until March 2009, well after the election.

In the primaries, Clinton – then the senator from New York with a long, distinguished record of public service – faced off against the relatively new face of the Democratic Party, Barack Obama.

Compared to Obama, Clinton had some significant drawbacks. For one, she represented the Washington establishment that so many Americans had come to despise. She had also voted for Bush's disastrous war in Iraq, which alienated progressives.

As one of only a few women to run in the primaries for a major-party ticket, she was subjected to a level of criticism that no male candidate would be. Her clothing, her ankles, her voice, were scrutinized meticulously. She was put in the same kind of no-win situation many women endure: if she acted reserved, she was labeled "cold." If she showed any feelings, she was labeled "overly emotional." As a candidate competing for the highest office in the land – arguably the most powerful position in the world – she was expected not to seem too ambitious.

But beneath all of that, she had the added baggage of decades of right-wing smears, accusations, and conspiracy theories. As Nazi propagandist Joseph Goebbels noted, "Repeat a lie often enough and it becomes the truth." The accusations and smears had been repeated almost daily on Fox News, the *Rush Limbaugh Show*, and countless other right-wing media outlets, newsletters, and websites, to the point where even many Democrats held the belief that she was somehow untrustworthy.

Nevertheless, it was a close race right up until the end. Once enough superdelegates threw their support behind Obama, it was clear that Clinton couldn't win, and she suspended her campaign in June.

Obama went on to win the general election in November, becoming the first Black man elected as president of the United States. As part of his attempt to build a broad coalition, he offered Clinton the role of Secretary of State, and she accepted.

But despite Obama's efforts to reach out to those on the other side of the aisle, there were too many who just would not accept him as their president.

Just weeks after his historic inauguration, the Tea Party was launched. While it appeared to be a grassroots movement of Americans who were tired of being, in their words, "Taxed Enough Already," in reality, it was an astroturfed political operation funded primarily by the Kochs through their super PACs Americans For Prosperity and FreedomWorks.[22]

And though the Tea Party was supposedly formed to protest the bailout of bankers in the fallout of the 2008 crash (while Republican George W. Bush was president), their anger wasn't directed at the crooked bankers or the corrupt politicians who bailed them out. Instead, their ire was aimed at the usual right-wing scapegoats: immigrants, welfare recipients, and government "bureaucrats," i.e., Democrats.[23] The Tea Party instantly attracted followers from the furthest fringes of the right: anti-government militia groups, the John Birch Society, the Council of Conservative Citizens, and others in the online world of the alt-right. Starting literally the day after Obama was elected in 2008, hate crimes against racial and ethnic minorities had skyrocketed, and over the following eight years, white supremacist groups saw a huge wave in recruitment, prompting the Department of Homeland Security to issue a report warning that the greatest terrorism threats were no longer from Al Qaeda, but from home-grown domestic extremist groups.

Much like the report released by Attorney General Janet Reno after the Oklahoma City bombing – which also warned of the danger of right-wing extremist groups – the report was met with howls of indignation from the GOP and right-wing media, accusing the authors of painting all conservatives as terrorists.

And just as the Clinton Administration did with Reno's report, the Obama Administration apologized and withdrew the report, and reassigned agents and funding away from the domestic terrorism threat to focus instead on Al Qaeda and Islamist threats.

But despite his capitulation, the Tea Party's hate remained focused on Obama. Racist effigies, signs, and memes circulated throughout Tea Party rallies and social media groups. He was frequently lynched in effigy, and shooting – or blowing up – targets with his face on them was a common pastime.

Many of them believed the conspiracy theories that he was a secret Muslim, or that he wasn't born in America, and thereby was unqualified to be president. This particular conspiracy theory would come to be called "birtherism," and one of its biggest – and loudest – proponents was Donald Trump. In spreading this conspiracy theory, Trump was making common cause with racists and white supremacists in the Tea Party. Which shouldn't be surprising; Trump's father, Fred, had once marched with the KKK, and Donald himself had a record of discriminating against Black people in his rental properties. People who worked with him on *The Apprentice* said he routinely threw around the n-word.

And now, the Tea Party – and the GOP generally – had a new avenue to attack their opponents. The internet and social media had become a part of everyday life, and for some, their only source of news and information. This created a new pipeline of bullshit. First, anonymous users would post smears and allegations against Obama or other Democrats (usually Hillary Clinton) on anonymous message boards like 4chan or, later, 8chan. Conspiracy theorists like Alex Jones, Glenn Beck, and Rush Limbaugh, who had huge platforms, would then repeat (and embellish) those claims, which would then get picked up by more respectable right-wing media outlets like Fox News, where hosts like Tucker Carlson would amplify them even further, platforming and legitimizing white nationalist beliefs like the great replacement theory. Disinformation researcher Melissa Ryan calls this the "4chan to Fox pipeline."[24]

Because the Tea Party's attacks on Obama and Democrats served the right's political agenda, this astroturfed group of patriot cosplayers was covered as though they were a legitimate movement by right-wing media – as well as mainstream media who were desperate to avoid being accused of "liberal bias."

***

Only a couple of months after Obama's historic inauguration, the Supreme Court heard oral arguments in

Citizens United v. Federal Election Commission. Attorneys representing the FEC argued that it had the authority to prohibit books or movies created by corporations. This led to heated discussion about the First Amendment, and so a new hearing was scheduled to decide the constitutionality of that underlying premise.

On January 21, 2010, in a five-to-four decision split along ideological lines, the conservatives on the Supreme Court ruled that the government could not ban political spending by corporations in candidate elections. They justified this by categorizing campaign spending as First Amendment-protected freedom of speech – and by defining corporations as "persons" that were entitled to exercise that right.

This decision overturned two previous precedents that upheld restrictions on corporate spending to support or oppose political candidates and that restricted campaign spending by corporations and unions.[25]

The dissenters – justices John Paul Stevens, Stephen G. Breyer, Ruth Bader Ginsburg, and Sonia Sotomayor – presciently warned that the court "had committed a grave error in treating corporate speech the same as that of human beings" and that "allowing corporate money to flood the political marketplace would corrupt democracy."[26]

And they were right. Every election cycle since the *Citizens United* ruling has seen record-breaking spending: according to CampaignLegal.org, spending by corporations and other outside groups increased by nearly nine hundred percent between 2008 and 2016.[27]

Among other things, the *Citizens United* ruling cleared the way for the creation of so-called super PACs, which, by law, can accept unlimited contributions from nearly any non-foreign source and spend unlimited amounts to influence the outcome of federal elections.[28] And though, on paper, these super PACs are supposed to report their donors, they are able to shield them behind donor organizations, which are not required to disclose who their donors are – i.e., "dark money." This dark money can come from anyone, anywhere – in the world.

ENDNOTES:

1. Victimsvoice, "If not for Mike Huckabee... Carol Sue Shields would be with us," YouTube, January 1, 2008. 0:57.

2. Linda Rosencrance, "Former Ark. governor hit with ethics complaint over destroyed hard drives." *Computerworld*, February 2, 2007.

3. Rosencrance, "Former Ark. governor."

4. Rosencrance, "Former Ark. governor."

5. Mike Huckabee, *Do the Right Thing: Inside the Movement That's Bringing Common Sense Back to America* (New York, New York: Penguin Group, 2008). p. 61.

6. Wolf Blitzer, CNN, December 7, 2007.

7. Blitzer, CNN.

8. Blitzer, CNN.

9. Blitzer, CNN.

10. McKay Coppins, "Here's The "Willie Horton" Ad Romney Almost Ran Against Mike Huckabee," *BuzzFeed News*, January 22, 2015.

11. *Hillary: The Movie*, directed by Alan Peterson (2008; Washington, D.C.: Citizens United). 0:00:16 – 0:00:33.

12. *Hillary: The Movie,* 0:01:02 – 0:01:06.

13. *Hillary: The Movie*, 0:01:06 – 0:01:14.

14. David Brock, *Blinded by the Right: The Conscience of an Ex-Conservative* (New York, New York: Three Rivers Press, 2003) p. 216.

15. Brock, *Blinded by the Right.*

16. Brock, *Blinded by the Right,* pp. 216-217.

17. Brock, *Blinded by the Right.*

18. Robert Barnes, "'Hillary: The Movie' to Get Supreme Court Screening," *The Washington Post*, March 15, 2009.

19. Barnes, "'Hillary: The Movie.'"

20. Barnes, "'Hillary: The Movie.'"

21. Barnes, "'Hillary: The Movie.'"

22. Joe Conason, *The Longest Con: How Grifters, Swindlers, and Frauds Hijacked American Conservatism* (New York, New York: St. Martin's Press, 2024) p. 150.

23. Conason, *Longest Con*, pp. 152-153.

24. Shannon Bond, "How Tucker Carlson took fringe conspiracy theories to a mass audience," *Morning Edition*, April 25, 2023.

25. Adam Liptak, "Justices, 5-4, Reject Corporate Spending Limit," *The New York Times*, January 21, 2010.

26. Liptak, "Justices, 5-4."

27. Georgia Lyon, "How Does the Citizens United Decision Still Affect Us in 2024?" CampaignLegal.org, January 24, 2024.

28. Lyon, "How Does the Citizens."

Chapter 13: "Lock Her Up"

It was Sunday, October 9, 2016, and the stage at Washington University in St. Louis was decked out in blue for the second presidential debate between Hillary Clinton and Donald Trump.

As Clinton worked the stage, answering questions from moderators Anderson Cooper and Martha Radditz, Trump followed her around, frequently standing near and slightly behind her, his face glowering, looking down on her with contempt. Pundits described it as "menacingly stalking" and "creepy," a specific kind of threatening behavior that many women recognized from their own experiences. Clinton would later say his "breathing down my neck" made her skin crawl.

When the question of Hillary's emails came up, Trump said that if he won, he would instruct his attorney general to "get a special prosecutor to look into your situation because there has never been so many lies, so much deception..."[1]

He continued blasting her for deleting and "acid washing" her emails – referring to thousands of her personal emails that she had deleted after turning over the official ones to the State Department in 2013, after she left office.

At the end of his diatribe, he said to Clinton, "You ought to be ashamed of yourself."[2]

In response, Clinton fact-checked him: "Everything he just said is absolutely false."[3] She went on to talk about how much he lies, and she encouraged the audience to fact-check him themselves. She then said, "You know, it is just awfully good that someone with the temperament of Donald Trump is not in charge of the law in our country."[4]

Trump interrupted her: "Because you'd be in jail."[5] The audience erupted in cheers.

***

From the time he rode down the gold escalator at Trump Tower to announce his presidency in June of 2015, Donald Trump had capitalized on the two strongest motivating factors for voters on the right: racism and the belief that Democrats – especially Hillary Clinton – were uniquely criminal and evil.

First, Trump's campaign heavily relied on exploiting racist resentment that, while always simmering below the surface, had boiled over after the election of Barack Obama. Trump's main platform plank, if it can be called that, was racist xenophobia. His announcement speech, which many in the mainstream media treated like a publicity stunt (because, in all likelihood, it was), was almost entirely focused on racist, nativist vitriol. The "nut graf," as they say in journalism, was when he went off script and said, "When Mexico sends its people, they're not sending their best," as though the thousands of migrants arriving at the southern border were being "sent" by Mexico. "They're bringing drugs," he continued. "They're bringing crime. They're rapists. And some, I assume, are good people."

With that speech, Trump signaled his full embrace of the furthest fringes of the right. But the other major factor (besides racism) that fueled Trump's campaign was his exploitation of the right's long-standing hatred of Hillary Clinton. With the help of the new 4chan-to-Fox pipeline, the conspiracy theories that had sprung up to smear the Clintons in the '90s had continued to grow and metastasize.

These wild allegations were repeated so often, for so long, that they just became true in the minds of their viewers and listeners. When she declared her candidacy for the presidency for the second time, in April of 2015, Hillary was still dealing with the years-long "scandal" of Benghazi, and the recent offshoot of that, her use of a private email server.

The Benghazi scandal erupted in 2012, while she was Secretary of State. On September 11 of that year, a terrorist attack on the U.S. State Department office in Benghazi, Libya, resulted in the deaths of four people, including two U.S. diplomats. This tragedy was immediately seized by the GOP to attack both Obama and Clinton. Mitt Romney, Obama's opponent in the presidential election, publicly claimed that Obama's first actions hadn't been to condemn the attacks, but to sympathize with the terrorists. No matter that none of that was true.[6] The narrative on the right shaped up quickly after that: Obama and Clinton had been criminally negligent in not supplying more security for the Benghazi offices, and now they were lying and engaging in a massive cover-up to hide their failures. To further that narrative, the GOP (which, thanks to the flood of corporate money enabled by *Citizens United,* had swept the House in the 2010 midterms) launched multiple investigations into what was now just being called "Benghazi." Clinton, to her credit, always cooperated, turning over anything requested and sitting for hours for questioning.

Like the Whitewater investigations of the '90s, the purpose of the Benghazi hearings wasn't to find the truth about what happened, but to provide right-wing media with plenty of soundbites and headlines designed to paint Clinton as guilty of *something*. It also provided the perfect excuse for GOP operatives to get in front of the cameras (or on the record) to attack Clinton, who was widely expected to be the next Democratic presidential candidate. Newt Gingrich appeared on Fox News to spread the lie that there had been jets ready to scramble and save the Americans in Benghazi, but the White House had told them to stand down.[7] Ryan Zinke, Republican representative from Montana, called her the anti-Christ during one of his campaign speeches.[8] The seventh and final Benghazi hearing was launched in 2014, clearly designed to be stretched out through the 2016 election cycle. Republican House majority leader Kevin McCarthy admitted as much in a "gaffe" reported in the *Washington Post*: "Everybody thought Hillary Clinton was unbeatable, right? But we put together a Benghazi special committee, a select committee. What are her numbers today? Her numbers are dropping."[9]

Despite all these investigations, though, Clinton was never found to have engaged in any wrongdoing. But the GOP did dig up something else they could use: while she was Secretary of State, she had used a private email server, a fairly common practice among many administration officials. When she left office in 2013, she had done a review of all her archived emails to determine which were her personal emails and which were "official" and belonged to the State Department. About 55,000 emails were determined to be official and were turned over to the government. The rest were supposed to be destroyed.

But the technician who was hired to destroy them had mistakenly left them intact. When the information about her using a private server surfaced, he went back to check his work and discovered his mistake. On his own initiative, he immediately deleted them using software called "BleachBit."[10] While it wasn't illegal or unethical, it did give the appearance of trying to cover something up. Fox News and the rest of the right-wing media – as well as the more "legit" press like the *New York Times* – beat the drum about her "email scandal" daily, devoting hundreds of minutes of airtime and inches of columns in print. The email scandal, more than anything else, would define her candidacy.

On the other side of the aisle, the 2016 Republican presidential primaries were much more crowded and held a lot more star power. Seventeen candidates filed to run in the GOP primaries, including Ted Cruz, Marco Rubio, Jeb Bush, and Rand Paul. The lesser-known candidates included John Kasich, Carly Fiorino, Ben Carson, and once again, Mike Huckabee.

Then there was the wild card, Donald Trump. He had no experience in government or public service, or within the Republican Party, or even in right-wing media generally. But he was a minor celebrity, thanks to hosting *The Apprentice* on NBC for twelve years. In the show, he was portrayed as a successful business mogul who would judge contestants on their supposed business acumen. Whenever a contestant was eliminated, he would utter his catchphrase, "You're fired."

It was all artifice, of course. Trump had been born into wealth, but had bankrupted nearly every business he had launched – including casinos. The one thing he was good at, though, was selling. Mostly, himself. His most – maybe only – successful gig was licensing his name to things other people built or sold. From high-rise buildings to bottled water, the "Trump" brand was supposed to confer high-status luxury – even though most of the products he hawked were cheap, low-quality crap, and in some cases, like Trump University, outright frauds. So in 2012, Republican dirty trickster and long-time Trump associate Roger Stone convinced him that he should run for president.[11]

That summer, Trump invited Jerry Falwell, Jr. and several other Evangelical leaders to a meeting at Trump Tower in New York City. There, Jerry Jr. had praised Trump as "one of the most influential political leaders in the United States," and the man who had forced Obama to release his birth certificate.[12]

With encouragement from Jerry Jr. and Roger Stone, in June of 2015, Trump rode down the gold-colored escalator at Trump Tower in New York City and, in front of the media and a small crowd of actors recruited off Craigslist, announced he was running for president.

He was nothing like anything the GOP had seen before. On the primary debate stages, he shouted over his competitors, called them names, and even alluded to the size of his own penis ("I guarantee you there's no problem. I guarantee.").

But he was clearly the crowd favorite. At the first debate, ABC's Dan Harris declared, "It was the Donald Trump show." His insults and bluster often brought cheers and applause from the audience.

The Tea Party was all in for him, and his candidacy "ingested the movement whole, scarcely pausing to burp..."[13] Amy Kremer, one of its founders, said of the Tea Party, "We just grew and morphed into something bigger and better – the MAGA movement."[14]

His political star had risen thanks to his promotion of the racist "birtherism" conspiracy theory, and nearly every speech he delivered was peppered with racist and/or nativist talking points that either alluded to or were copied straight from white supremacist social media. This led to Tea Party/MAGA followers insisting that Trump, a compulsive liar, "tells it like it is" – meaning, like the posters, podcasters, and YouTubers who make up the information bubble of the terminally online alt-right.

Despite his support from Jerry Falwell, Jr. and other Evangelical leaders, rank and file Evangelicals had no use for this crass, dishonest, and obviously non-religious candidate. That was made painfully clear at the Values Voter

Summit in September 2015. When he called Marco Rubio a clown, instead of the expected laughs and applause, Trump got only boos from the deeply conservative audience. In the straw poll afterwards, he only got five percent of the vote.[15]

So, in an effort to shore up his support from fundamentalist Christians, one of the most powerful constituencies – if not the most powerful – in the Republican Party, Trump again hosted a meeting with some of their leaders in Trump Tower. This time, almost forty ministers met with him, including televangelists Kenneth Copeland and Paula White (White would go on to become Trump's spiritual adviser). Many, if not all, of them were members of a movement called the New Apostolic Reformation, the newest version of Christian nationalist Dominionism ideology. They base much of their beliefs and tactics on something called the Seven Mountains Mandate, or 7M, and which takes its name from several Biblical verses that use "mountains" as metaphors for seats of power. Their core belief is that Christians (specifically conservative, white, Evangelical Christians) need to take over the "seven mountains" of society – family, religion, education, news media, the arts, business, and government – in order to establish the Kingdom of God on Earth. The movement is heavily influenced by charismatic denominations like Pentecostalism, so speaking in tongues, faith healing, and prophesying are common practices. The 7M movement had been floating around conservative Christian circles since the 1970s, but got its big boost in 2013 with the publication of *Invading Babylon: The 7 Mountain Mandate* by Bill Johnson and Lance Wallnau.

By the time these Dominionist Evangelical leaders met with Trump in 2015, the movement's talking points had moved up the pipeline of bullshit to Glenn Beck's show, and its adherents were found throughout the religious right's media ecosphere of televangelists, podcasters, and YouTubers. At their meeting with Trump, they laid hands on him and beseeched God to protect and guide him in his mission to save America.[16]

Afterwards, they would go on to not only praise Trump from the pulpit (in violation of their tax-exempt status), but claim to prophesy about him and his enemies. They amplified and elaborated on the existing Evangelical mythology about Democrats, where they were evil degenerates, killing babies, worshiping Satan, and hell-bent on wiping Christians off the face of the earth.

But these new Dominionists now had a savior. According to them, Trump was a fallen "King Cyrus" figure, chosen by God to cast out these dark, evil forces of Satan from the Deep State.

Many people in the media, and on Main Street, were perplexed at this phenomenon of fundamentalist Christians being so supportive of a lying, braggadocious, adulterous fraudster who did not appear to have even a basic grasp of the tenets of Christianity. For example, he called the Book of Second Corinthians "Two Corinthians." When asked about his favorite Bible verse – almost every Christian's favorite thing to talk about – he squirmed out of answering, claiming, "It's very personal."

But none of that really mattered to the Dominionists who supported him (including Mike Huckabee, who had dropped out of the race after a poor showing in the Iowa Caucuses). As Joe Conason puts it in his book *The Longest Con*, Trump attracted "the religious leaders most inclined toward grift and greed (not unlike Trump himself) ..."[17] Conason says that what drew them in was "how much he resembled the televangelists who were the most successful among them. ... they had much in common. His unbridled pursuit of wealth, his disdain for government, and his propensity to make extravagant promises with no means or intention of fulfilling them echoed the lifestyle of a top-tier prosperity preacher."[18]

To the shock of a lot of Beltway pundits, Trump won the Republican Party nomination. But to a lot of people out in flyover country, it was no surprise. Here was now, finally, a candidate who reflected back at them the same grievances and conspiracy theories they had been stewing in for decades – especially about Hillary Clinton.

In fact, besides racism, the Trump campaign's other major "plank" was that Clinton was so corrupt, so criminal, and so evil that she represented an existential threat to the United States.

His attacks on her ran the gamut from the garden-variety sexism of criticizing her looks to the party-line allegations of criminality involving her handling of Benghazi and her emails, both of which the mainstream media were only too willing to amplify.

But he also threw red meat to his base by repeating some of the tinfoil-hat conspiracy theories that had been simmering in the fringes of the right since the '90s, like the Clinton Body Count, as well as the newest one, Pizzagate, and its central lie that the Clintons are pedophiles.

Meanwhile, Clinton was being held to a much higher standard. In one of her biggest controversies, she was caught on tape talking with donors and describing half of Trump supporters as a "basket of deplorables." Even though she was describing "racist, sexist, homophobic, xenophobic, Islamophobic" people – who are objectively deplorable – she was roundly criticized by the pearl-clutching Beltway chattering class.

Never mind that Republicans, since the days of Newt Gingrich (and Evangelicals, since the '80s), have been calling Democrats – all Democrats – Communists, traitors, baby killers, degenerates, perverts, pedophiles, criminals, liars, psychopaths, and on and on.

For decades, the right had cultivated an entire media ecosystem – from mimeographed church newsletters to AM talk radio shows, to blogs, podcasts, and TV networks – dedicated to spreading right-wing views and talking points. They built, brick by brick, year after year, the narrative that the left, and by extension, Democrats, are less moral, honest, and patriotic than Republicans. Republicans, the party consistently aligned with the interests of big business, are portrayed as representing "real Americans," with the implication that Democrats don't – either because the Americans who vote Democratic aren't "real" Americans, or else that the Democrats don't represent Americans at all, but only some fabled "liberal elite" or "shadowy globalists" or whatever Communist country we're currently hating. The former narrative, especially, was taken up by the Christian right and spun out into an entire mythology.

The candidacy of Donald Trump was the inevitable culmination of the right's ever-more-radical rhetoric. He's called women "nasty," Black folks "low IQ," and the media "the enemies of the people." He calls Democrats "the radical left," "people who hate our country," "criminals," "traitors," and more. His supporters would often sport T-shirts, hats, and other merch with messages like "Trump That Bitch," "Hillary Sucks, But Not Like Monica," and "Hillary for Prison." His supporters called her "Killary" and circulated images of her with blood dripping off her hands. At his Nuremberg-style campaign rallies, Trump frequently led his crowds in chanting, "Lock her up!"

Far more concerning, he often hinted at – or outright called for – violence. At a rally in North Carolina, he told his crowd that if Clinton won, she would be able to pick judges, and "there's nothing you can do, folks," he said.

"Although the Second Amendment people — maybe there is, I don't know." His campaign insisted he only meant that gun owners should "unite against Clinton this fall," but the implication was clear.[19] When Al Baldasaro, an unofficial campaign adviser who frequently shared a stage with Trump, said Clinton "should be put in the firing line and shot for treason," Trump's campaign spokesperson, Hope Hicks, only said that Trump "did not agree with his comments." The Trump campaign didn't sever ties with him, and in fact, continued to welcome him onstage at rallies.[20] Roger Stone, who had urged Trump to run and long been in his innermost circle of advisers, tweeted that Clinton "must be brought to justice — arrested, tried, and executed for murder."[21] But the violent rhetoric – and actions – weren't just targeted at Hillary Clinton. Trump frequently called for his supporters to "rough up" protesters at his rallies. "Knock the crap out of him, would you?" he said, promising to pay the attackers' legal fees. And unsurprisingly, several attacks on protesters and journalists took place at his rallies.

The effects of his violent rhetoric spilled out further: a *Washington Post* study found that counties that had hosted a Trump campaign rally saw a 226 percent increase in reported hate crimes over comparable counties that did not host a rally.[22]

Because Clinton was consistently leading in the polls, many people, including many journalists, continued to treat Trump's campaign as just a publicity stunt. As a former reality-TV star, he had the kind of showmanship that journalists can't resist. He drew views and clicks, and they gave him anywhere from $2 billion to $6 billion in what was essentially free advertising.

He also had a lot of help behind the scenes, too. By the time he was cast in *The Apprentice*, he had been blacklisted by almost every bank in North America, and was increasingly reliant on laundered money.[23] In 2014, during a conversation with golf writer James Dodson, Eric Trump off-handedly admitted that "We have all the funding we need out of Russia." It was no secret that Russia opposed Clinton and recognized it would be to their advantage to have someone in the White House who owed them in some way. As far back as the primaries, accounts traced to Russia and former Soviet republics had been flooding social media with anti-Clinton messaging, which were then promoted as "news" on Facebook and Twitter.[24] Posts with the most outrageous, frightening lies about Clinton were shared the most, generating the most revenue.[25] Russia also spent millions to campaign against Clinton – and for Trump – using paid "troll farms" and targeted advertising on Facebook.[26]

Then, during a rambling press conference on July 27 where he criticized Clinton for not holding press conferences (among other things), Trump said, "Russia, if you're listening, I hope you're able to find the 30,000 emails that are missing. I think you will probably be rewarded mightily by our press." An investigation would later uncover that on or around that same time, Russia did, in fact, target the Clinton campaign's email addresses with spear-phishing attacks.

The attacks were part of "a sophisticated, large-scale hacking effort by twelve Russian officers to interfere with the 2016 elections by stealing documents from private servers and staging their release through fake online personas, such as Guccifer 2.0 and DCLeaks," according to PBS' reporting on the indictments.[27]

The biggest, or at least most consequential, of these email dumps took place in early October, immediately after the leak of the *Access Hollywood* tape, where Trump is heard bragging that he can "grab 'em by the pussy." That kind of bombshell would tank the candidacy of any other candidate, but the release of thousands of emails from Clinton's campaign manager, John Podesta, sucked all the air out of the room – and sparked the conspiracy theory that would quickly morph into Pizzagate.

Caving to public pressure to investigate the newly released emails, FBI Director James Comey – the former deputy special counsel to the Senate Whitewater Committee that had investigated the Clintons in the '90s – decided to break with Bureau policy and announced, just eleven days before the election, that he would be reopening the previously closed investigation into Clinton's mishandling of emails.[28]

Each of these scandals resulted in a hit to Clinton's poll numbers, but she was still ahead of Trump right up until Election Day. In the end, she earned nearly three million more votes than he did. But thanks to the uniquely undemocratic way the United States chooses our presidents, those votes weren't from the "right" – i.e., rural – states. Because he was so widely supported in those smaller, redder states, Trump garnered more Electoral College votes – 304 to 227 – thereby winning the presidency.

ENDNOTES:

1. *PBS NewsHour*, "Watch the second presidential debate between Hillary Clinton and Donald Trump," YouTube video, October 9, 2016. 0:22:29.

2. *PBS NewsHour*, "Watch," 0:23:29.

3. *PBS NewsHour*, "Watch," 0:23:35.

4. *PBS NewsHour*, "Watch," 0:24:12.

5. *PBS NewsHour*, "Watch," 0:24:19.

6. Michael D'Antonio, *The Hunting of Hillary: The Forty-Year Campaign to Destroy Hillary Clinton* (New York, New York: St. Martin's Press, 2020) p. 225.

7. D'Antonio, *Hunting of Hillary*, p. 227.

8. D'Antonio, *Hunting of Hillary*, p. 221.

9. D'Antonio, *Hunting of Hillary*, p. 228.

10. D'Antonio, *Hunting of Hillary*, p. 246.

11. Conason, *Longest Con*, pp. 196-197.

12. Conason, *Longest Con*, p. 187.

13. Conason, *Longest Con*, p. 161.

14. Conason, *Longest Con*, p. 162.

15. Conason, *Longest Con*, p. 191.

16. Conason, *Longest Con*.

17. Conason, *Longest Con*, p. 189.

18. Conason, *Longest Con*, pp. 189, 192.

19. Michael Crowley, "Trump's long dalliance with violent rhetoric," Politico.com, August 10, 2016.

20. Crowley, "Trump's long dalliance."

21. Crowley, "Trump's long dalliance."

22. Ayal Feinberg, Regina Branton, and Valerie Martinez-Ebers, "Counties that hosted a 2016 Trump rally saw a 226 percent increase in hate crimes," *The Washington Post*, March 22, 2019.

23. Conason, Longest Con, pp. 205-206.

24. D'Antonio, *Hunting of Hillary*, p. 264.

25. D'Antonio, *Hunting of Hillary*, p. 265.

26. D'Antonio, *Hunting of Hillary*, p. 267.

27. Erica R. Hendry, "Trump asked Russia to find Clinton's emails. On or around the same day, Russia targeted her accounts," *PBS News*, July 13, 2018.

28. D'Antonio, *Hunting of Hillary*, p. 279.

Chapter 14: Washington, D.C.

Starting early that frosty January morning, supporters of President Donald Trump began gathering at the Ellipse at the Capitol Mall to hear him speak. They'd come from all around the country, heeding their president's call to come to the Capitol on January 6 to "stop the steal" and "take our country back." Some flew in, some drove, some carpooled, and some rode in on chartered buses.

Even before any ballots had been cast, Trump had been telling the American people that the election of 2020 would be "rigged." And when he lost, he kept repeating his claims, even though he knew they were false, that the election had been stolen from him, and by extension, from them. Their enemies – the Deep State Democrats – had done this through thousands of fraudulent mail-in ballots, or else the voting machines had been hacked to switch votes from Trump to Biden, or else boxes of ballots for Trump had been dumped in the trash, or any of a dozen other unfounded conspiracy theories.

Trump and his surrogates on social media and right-wing TV networks like Fox, OAN, and Newsmax had been beating the drum for months, promising they had conclusive evidence that the election had been stolen – but they were never able to produce any of it. Trump's lawyers had filed over sixty court cases to try and overturn the election results in key battleground states; every one of them had failed.

But for the faithful, facts were not important. Many of his supporters – especially Evangelicals – had come to be outright hostile to facts and science, as demonstrated by their widespread, sometimes violent, refusal of public health measures in the face of the COVID-19 pandemic.

No, his supporters "knew" he had won the same way they knew that these were the End Days: because their preachers and leaders had told them so. They had seen it in visions.

Even before he was elected in 2016, dozens of New Apostolic Reformation and similarly aligned Dominionist preachers and self-proclaimed prophets had anointed Trump as the leader chosen by God. As such, they predicted, he could only win again in 2020.[1] This idea was circulated through podcasts, social media, and the pulpits of hard-right Evangelical preachers and televangelists like Kenneth Copeland, Hank Kunneman, Kat Kerr, Greg Locke, and dozens of others.

Indeed, Evangelicals, fundamentalists, and other Christian nationalists were well represented among the crowd on January 6. Besides the many Christian flags, supporters waved signs depicting Jesus wearing a red MAGA hat, wore T-shirts proclaiming "Jesus is my savior; Trump is my president," and held aloft crosses and Bibles.

There were other flags being flown, including the militia movement's Gadsden flag and Confederate flag. Some flew the flags of known terrorist groups like the Proud Boys, Three Percenters, and the Oath Keepers. But there was a new symbol showing up on flags, signs, and T-shirts that day: the letter Q.

The QAnon phenomenon is difficult to explain. In his docuseries *Into the Storm*, director Cullen Hoback describes QAnon (the phenomenon, not the 4chan poster) as part interactive game, part religion, and part political movement.

It started in mid-October of 2017 with an anonymous post on one of 4chan's message boards. The poster, Q, claimed to be a high-ranking government official with a "Q-level" security clearance, and they were posting allegedly highly classified government information.

But the posts weren't information, really. They were mostly collections of short, cryptic phrases and/or a series of open-ended questions. For example, Q's second post (referred to as a "Q drop") reads, in part:

"Mockingbird.

HRC detained, not arrested (yet).

Where is Huma? Follow Huma.

This has nothing to do w/ Russia (yet)."

And so on. (The reference to Huma is likely referring to Huma Abedin, Hillary Clinton's longtime aide and chair of her 2016 campaign who was frequently named in the leaked DNC email scandal).

Like the writings of Nostradamus, Q drops could be interpreted in an infinite number of ways, and literally any detail could be taken as "confirmation." The vagueness of the posts, and allusions to existing conspiracy theories, attracted conspiracy-minded people to "connect the dots" (as they put it) and draw conclusions based on nothing more than sloppy pattern-recognition. This "connecting the dots" led to the rise of a class of "bakers" – bloggers, vloggers, podcasters, and YouTubers who drew huge followings "translating" and discussing Q drops, tying them into events in the news or Biblical prophecies.[2]

Subsequent Q drops would sometimes reference those translations, suggesting a kind of feedback loop between the followers and whoever Q was (Hoback believes it's 8kun administrator Ron Watkins).

These translations and discussions coalesce around a set of beliefs which could best be understood as an offshoot of New Apostolic Reformation beliefs, amped up with a heavy dose of conspiracy theories. In fact, QAnon has been called the "uber-conspiracy theory," in that it incorporates nearly every other conspiracy theory through history, from the centuries-old antisemitic accusations of "blood libel," to flat earth theories, to belief that coronavirus vaccines are really a secret way for Bill Gates to implant humanity with microscopic tracking devices.

But the central belief that all the others lead to is just Pizzagate 2.0, which itself was just an amped-up version of the myths that fundamentalist Evangelicals have been pushing about the left since the 1980s. QAnon followers literally believe that hundreds of celebrities and Democrats are part of a cabal of Satanists engaged in child sex trafficking, murder, and cannibalism – specifically, harvesting and drinking "adrenochrome." Hillary Clinton figures prominently in it; if the QAnon universe were a video game, she would be the final boss. Followers also believe that Trump was, and still is, waging a secret war against these Deep State enemies, and one day, he will have them all arrested and publicly executed in an apocalyptic event they call "the storm."

QAnon moved from the dark corners of the internet and into the wider world when, in December of 2017, Alex Jones hosted Jerome Corsi, fellow right-wing conspiracy theorist and *Infowars'* Washington, D.C., "bureau chief." The title of the show was "The Secrets of QAnon's War With the Deep State, Pedophiles Exposed."

From there, QAnon burst into social media fame, spreading via viral memes and clips. And thanks to Facebook's and YouTube's algorithms, thousands of people were funneled into the rabbit hole of QAnon conspiracy theories. The shutdowns in 2020 gave QAnon a shot in the arm – pun intended – when millions of people were stuck indoors with little to no human contact. Many turned to the internet and social media to find community, especially if that community could help them make sense of something as frightening as the coronavirus pandemic.

And while some of QAnon's new recruits came from wellness and anti-vaccine corners of the left, the movement was clearly right-wing – and was immediately embraced by the GOP. Key members of Trump's administration openly displayed their belief in (or support of) QAnon. Roger Stone and Steve Bannon frequently referred to QAnon talking points on podcasts and other public appearances. Retired general and Trump's national security adviser Mike Flynn was one of its biggest proponents, to the point of signing autographs with "WWG1WGA," an acronym for the QAnon battle cry, "Where We Go One, We Go All." And none were a bigger "get" for the movement than the president himself. Trump would frequently "wink" at QAnon, such as by pointing out people in his crowds sporting Q signs or T-shirts. He would repeat subtle references in speeches, and he retweeted Q-related posts and memes regularly. In August of 2020, when asked about QAnon, he said, "I don't know much about the movement other than I understand they like me very much, which I appreciate," before going on to say he had heard it was growing in popularity – the highest compliment Trump can give.[3] Two months later, during a time when Trump was retweeting a lot of Q-related posts, NBC's Savannah Guthrie asked him if he would state for the record that QAnon's conspiracy theories weren't true. Trump feigned ignorance, then when Guthrie explained the central tenet, he said, "they were very much against pedophilia" and that he supported that.[4]

By 2020, millions of people – fully half of Trump's base – believed in QAnon conspiracy theories.[5] Dozens of QAnon candidates ran for local, state, and federal offices that year; Marjorie Taylor Green and Lauren Boebert are the two most prominent among them.[6]

But on January 6, 2021, the mood among QAnon was tense. None of Q's predictions of a massive round-up of Deep State predators had come to pass, and their divinely ordained leader had apparently had the election stolen from him. For years they had been whipped into a righteous rage against Satanic forces who abused and killed children, and like any apocalyptic cult, they felt that if their prophesied Armageddon didn't happen on its own, they would have to make it happen. As one Q-Tuber put it, they were in a cold civil war against the left: "We will murder them all."[7] The FBI had picked up on this, too. A year earlier, the Bureau released a memo warning that the movement represented a significant domestic terrorist threat. But Trump's Homeland Security was instructed not to label QAnon or other violent right-wing extremist groups as "terrorists," and blocked funding and resources to track or investigate them.

On January 6, several speakers, including representatives Mo Brooks and Madison Cawthorn, as well as Trump lawyer Rudy Giuliani, addressed the crowds gathered on the Ellipse that morning. Each of them urged the crowd to "fight," "fight like hell," and "kick ass," to "save America."

Finally, their true leader, as ordained by God, took the podium. After a few minutes pointing out how many of them were there (and a few jabs at the "fake news"), he returned to the Big Lie, repeating that the election was rigged and stolen by the "radical left Democrats" and the "fake news media."

"We will never give up, we will never concede," he said at one point during his hour-long speech. Several minutes later, after yet more lies about how the election was fraudulent, he told the crowd, "We want to go back and we want to get this right because we're going to have somebody in there that should not be in there, and our country will be destroyed, and we're not going to stand for that." He told them they have to "fight like hell, or you won't have a country." And he directed them to march on the Capitol, which he had purposefully left vulnerable, with only a small contingency of the National Guard on hand to assist the D.C. Metropolitan police.

They did as he instructed, attacking officers and news media crews and smashing through windows to enter the Capitol building where, thankfully, Congress members had been whisked away to safety.

As they milled around the empty Capitol building, some of them engaged in acts of petty theft and vandalism, but others gathered in the Senate chamber. A group of four men, including the ridiculously costumed Jacob Chansley, dubbed the "QAnon shaman," took to the central dais. There Chansley, using a megaphone, led those gathered in a prayer. In it, he thanked the heavenly father for their God-given inalienable rights, among other things. Then, in a sentence that called to mind the one spoken by Rev. James Robison in 1980 that had launched the Moral Majority, merging Evangelical Christianity with the Republican Party, Chansley thanked his heavenly father for allowing them to "send a message to all the tyrants, the Communists, and the globalists, that this is our nation, not theirs."

After more than three hours – during which time he refused to call in the National Guard or any other protection for the Capitol building - Trump finally sent out a statement urging the rioters to go home, in "peace." Notably, he didn't condemn the violence, and he again repeated the lie that the election was fraudulent.

Later that night, after the building had been cleared, the House and Senate reconvened to finally certify the results of the election and declare Joe Biden the winner.

Several Republicans, including Lindsey Graham and Mitch McConnell, forcefully condemned Trump and the violence that he had unleashed on them. Finally, now, it seemed the GOP had come to its senses and seen the harm caused by their lies and conspiracy theories. Now, at long last, the nation could get back to normal.

ENDNOTES:

1. Julia Duin, "The Christian Prophets Who Say Trump Is Coming Again," Politico.com, February 18, 2021.

2. *Into the Storm*, Season 1, Episode 1: "Calm Before the Storm," Directed by Cullen Hoback, aired March 21, 2021, on HBO Max.

3. Maegan Vazquez, "Trump again refuses to denounce QAnon," CNN.com, October 15, 2020.

4. Vazquez, "Trump again refuses."

5. Colin Dickey, "From Sound of Freedom to Ron DeSantis: How QAnon's crazy conspiracy theories went mainstream," *The Guardian*, August 16, 2023.

6. *Into the Storm*, Season 1, Episode 6: "The Storm."

7. *Into the Storm*, Season 1, Episode 5: "Game Over."

Epilogue

In the wake of January 6, Facebook and Twitter blocked or suspended thousands of QAnon accounts, along with those of far-right groups and influencers and Trump himself.

The FBI investigation of the events of January 6 was the largest criminal investigation in the Bureau's history. Over 1,200 people were charged for their actions seeking to overturn the election that day, including nearly 600 people charged with assaulting police officers or members of the media.

In February 2021, Trump was impeached, for the second time, by the House of Representatives for inciting an insurrection. The Republican-controlled Senate, however, refused to convict him, thanks to Senate Majority Leader Mitch McConnell McConnell acknowledged that Trump was "practically and morally responsible" for the events of January 6, but he still voted not guilty. His reasoning was, since the punishment for conviction was removal from office, and Trump had already left office (thanks to McConnell's efforts to delay impeachment hearings), Trump was Constitutionally ineligible for conviction. McConnell justified his not guilty vote by assuring his colleagues and voters that Trump would now be subject to legal consequences, because, as he said, "former presidents are not immune."

But as time went by, the right wing began rewriting the events of that day, using a variety of conflicting lies.

Some claim that the rioters were really Antifa and/or FBI informants just trying to frame innocent Trump supporters. Some push the easily debunked lie that it was really Nancy Pelosi's fault, because Trump offered National Guard support, but Pelosi refused it. Others – including Trump – say that it wasn't even a riot at all, but a "day of love." At the same time, they call the January 6 rioters "patriots" and "political prisoners."

And as time went on, any hopes of bring Trump or his accomplices to justice were dashed, one by one.

First, Facebook and Twitter folded, reinstating insurrectionists' accounts. When billionaire Elon Musk purchased Twitter, he embarked on a project of turning one of the most popular social media sites into a megaphone for right-wing disinformation and conspiracy theories. He not only reinstated the accounts of Trump and other insurrectionists, but actively changed the algorithm to boost their posts.

On the legal front, Attorney General Merrick Garland slow-walked the investigations into Trump, only naming a special prosecutor into his many crimes – including inciting an insurrection on January 6 – in November 2022, after Trump announced he would be running for president again. Worse, when Trump's appeals of those court cases went before the Supreme Court – where three sitting justices had been appointed by him – they decided, in *Trump v. United States*, that presidents enjoy near-total immunity from prosecution. Then, in 2024, thanks to the Supreme Court's decision in *Trump v. Anderson,* the Fourteenth Amendment was tossed aside, and Trump, who had been impeached for inciting an insurrection, was able to run for president again.

To the shock of many, he won. And though he appeared to make inroads with certain demographics, like Latino and Black men, once again his strongest base of support came from the White Evangelical community: polls show that eight out of ten white Evangelicals supported him in this election (Jones, 2024).

This time around, he has fully embraced QAnon and its related conspiracy theories, even more so than before. He frequently refers to QAnon followers as "patriots" and uses QAnon words and phrases at his rallies, where he plays the "QAnon anthem" (a piece of stock music plagiarized from its actual composer). He has also promised to pardon the January 6 rioters.

Worse, he frequently repeats Nazi talking points, such as that the press and his political opponents are "the enemy within." He said immigrants are "poisoning the blood of the nation," and refers to them (as well as his "enemies") as "vermin." Among other dark and troubling promises, he has repeatedly vowed to execute mass deportations and have his Department of Justice investigate his political opponents.

Trump also says he will appoint wealthy conspiracy theorists to his cabinet, like Elon Musk – who frequently retweets great replacement theory and other Nazi talking points – and Robert F. Kennedy, Jr. – a wing-nut anti-vaxxer.

And, like a bad penny, Mike Huckabee has turned up yet again. Huckabee, as a Dominionist, is also a Zionist, believing Israel has a crucial part to play in the End Times, and that God will bless the nations who bless (i.e., give unconditional support to) Israel. Huckabee has been caught on tape saying that there is no such thing as Palestine, only Judea and Samaria, and he refuses to call illegal Israeli settlements in the occupied West Bank "settlements," but rather as simply "communities, neighborhoods, and cities." He opposes a two-state solution to the war. And, in a clear sop to the Christian nationalists who elected him, Trump has pledged to nominate Huckabee as ambassador to Israel.

As I write this, in late 2024, we do not know how this story will end. But we do know that the past is prologue. The allegations and conspiracy theories against the left, Democrats, and Hillary specifically have been festering in the basement of the American right for decades. QAnon simply took what was already there, amped it up, and spread it further than anyone thought possible. It directly led to the violence on January 6, and it hasn't let up since. I only hope that it doesn't succeed at what it attempted four years ago.

Photographs

Dusty Dumond. Courtesy of Special Collections, University of Arkansas Libraries, Fayetteville, Jack E. Hill Papers (MC 1968). Series 3, box 41, folder 32.

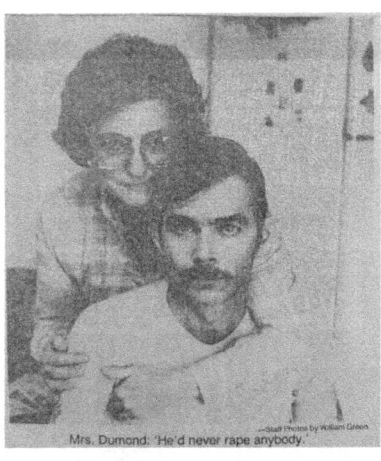

Wayne and Dusty Dumond. Photo credit: William Green/ Arkansas Gazette. Courtesy of Special Collections, University of Arkansas Libraries, Fayetteville, Jack E. Hill Papers (MC 1968). Series 3, box 41, folder 32.

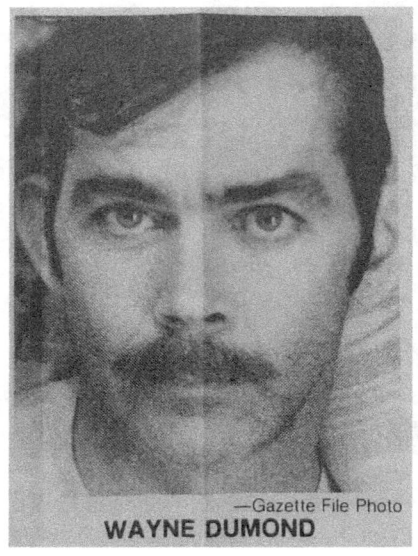

Wayne Dumond. Photo credit: Arkansas Gazette. Courtesy of Special Collections, University of Arkansas Libraries, Fayetteville, Jack E. Hill Papers (MC 1968). Series 3, box 41, folder 35.

Ashley Stevens. Photo credit: Arkansas Times. Courtesy of Special Collections, University of Arkansas Libraries, Fayetteville, Jack E. Hill Papers (MC 1968). Series 3, box 41, folder 38.

Carol Sue Shields. Photo credit: Arkansas Times. Courtesy of Special Collections, University of Arkansas Libraries, Fayetteville, Jack E. Hill Papers (MC 1968). Series 3, box 41, folder 38.

Coolidge Conlee. Photo credit: William Green/Arkansas Gazette.
Courtesy of Special Collections, University of Arkansas Libraries,
Fayetteville, Jack E. Hill Papers (MC 1968). Series 3, box 42, folder 4.

Jack Hill at typewriter. Courtesy of Special Collections,
University of Arkansas Libraries, Fayetteville, Jack E.
Hill Papers (MC 1968). Series 3, box 42, folder 32.

Acknowledgements

A project like this wouldn't happen without "standing on the shoulders of giants," and I could not have written this without the research done by much better researchers than myself: author Joe Conason, for his decades of research into the ways the right has vilified the Clintons; Randy Dixon, of the David and Barbara Pryor Center for Arkansas Oral and Visual History, for his immense depth of knowledge about the Wayne Dumond case and his generosity in sharing it with me; and Max Brantley, former editor of the *Arkansas Times*, for sharing his time and decades of experience with me. I credit them with everything I got right; any errors are mine alone.

I also owe an enormous debt of gratitude to the staff at the Fayetteville Public Library, as well as the Special Collections staff at Mullins Library at the University of Arkansas. I want to think Bryce Keaton, as well, whose video inspired me to dig deeper into the Wayne Dumond case in the first place.

I also want to thank my friends and family for their understanding while I sequestered myself in my office to finish this thing.

Finally, I want to thank my sweetheart, Richard, for keeping me fed and giving me all the time and quiet I needed to work. Thank you.

Bibliography

ABC News, "Huckabee Helped Set Rapist Free Who Later Killed Missouri Woman," November 30, 2009. https://abcnews.go.com/Blotter/mike-huckabee-clemency-freed-maurice-clemmons-washington-cop-shooter-suspect/story?id=9207095

Arango, Tim, "A 'Tabloid Guy' Calls It a Night After 41 Years With Murdoch," *New York Times,* September 28, 2008. https://www.nytimes.com/2008/09/29/business/media/29dunleavy.html?scp=2&sq=arkansas&st=cse

"Arkansas Prison Reform," The James Guy Tucker, Jr., Processing Blog. Center for Arkansas History and Culture, December 22, 2015. https://ualrexhibits.org/tuckerblog/2015/12/22/arkansas-prison-reform/

Associated Press, "Clinton Decides He Won't Seek '88 Nomination," *The New York Times*, July 15, 1987. https://www.nytimes.com/1987/07/15/us/clinton-decides-he-won-t-seek-88-nomination.html

"Audio/Video Spots," Save Our Nation. http://www.saveournation.net/spots.htm.

Ault, Larry, "Dumond ally implies Conlee knew of castration," *Arkansas Democrat*, August 9, 1988.

Barnes, Robert, "'Hillary: The Movie' to Get Supreme Court Screening," *The Washington Post*, March 15, 2009.

https://www.washingtonpost.com/wp-dyn/content/article/2009/03/14/AR2009031401603_pf.html

Bergeron, Josh, "D.C. pizza restaurant shooting suspect from Salisbury remains in jail on gun charges," *Salisbury Post*, December 6, 2016. https://www.salisburypost.com/2016/12/06/d-c-pizza-restaurant-shooter-salisbury-remains-jail-gun-charges/

Blomeley, Seth, "DuMond in news rekindles emotions," *Arkansas Democrat-Gazette*, December 9, 2007, p. 1,17. https://www.arkansasonline.com/news/2007/dec/09/dumond-news-rekindles-emotions-20071209/

Blumenthal, Max, "Is Huckabee Rapture Ready? And Why Did He Free A Born-Again Rapist? A Confidant Speaks," *The Huffington Post*, January 14, 2008.

Blumenthal, Max, "The Real Mike Huckabee," *The Nation*, January 28, 2008.

Bond, Shannon, "How Tucker Carlson took fringe conspiracy theories to a mass audience," *Morning Edition*, April 25, 2023. https://www.npr.org/2023/04/25/1171800317/how-tucker-carlsons-extremist-narratives-shaped-fox-news-and-conservative-politi

Brantley, Max, in discussion with the author, January 2021.

Brantley, Max, "Mike Huckabee's entry to 2016 campaign brings back Wayne Dumond," *Arkansas Times*, January 23, 2015.

Brantley, Max, "The dark side of Mike Huckabee," Salon.com, November 13, 2007. https://www.salon.com/2007/11/13/huckabee_5/

Brantley, Max, "The Dumond file – and more," *Arkansas Times*, December 5, 2007.

Brock, David, *Blinded by the Right: The Conscience of an Ex-Conservative*. New York, New York: Three Rivers Press, 2003.

Brown, Robert L., "Jim Guy Tucker," *Defining Moments: Historic Decisions by Arkansas Governors from McMath through Huckabee*, Fayetteville, Arkansas: The University of Arkansas Press, 2010. pp. 109-119.

Byrd, Dennis, "Conlee's trial holds ironic moment," *Arkansas Democrat*, November 8, 1988, p. 23.

Carpenter, Dale and Robert Cochran, *Reporting for Arkansas: The Documentary Films of Jack Hill*. Fayetteville, Arkansas: The University of Arkansas Press, 2022.

Cate, Matthew S.L., "DuMond case puts Huckabee in hot seat," *Arkansas Democrat-Gazette*, December 6, 2007. https://www.arkansasonline.com/news/2007/dec/06/dumond-case-puts-huckabee-hot-seat-20071206/

Chafets, Zev, "The Huckabee Factor," *The New York Times Magazine*, December 12, 2007. https://www.nytimes.com/2007/12/12/magazine/16huckabee.html

Clarkson, Frederick, "Anti-Abortion Movement Marches On After Two Decades of Arson, Bombs and Murder," *The Intelligence Report,* September 15, 1998. https://www.splcenter.org/fighting-hate/intelligence-report/1998/anti-abortion-movement-marches-after-two-decades-arson-bombs-and-murder

Clinton House Museum, "Bill Clinton," https://clintonhousemuseum.org/bill-clinton/

Clinton House Museum, "Timeline," https://clintonhousemuseum.org/timeline/

Cochran, Robert, "Jack Edward Hill," The Encyclopedia of Arkansas. https://encyclopediaofarkansas.net/entries/jack-edward-hill-12890/

Conason, Joe, *Big Lies: The Right-Wing Propaganda Machine and How It Distorts the Truth*. New York, New York: Thomas Dunne Books, 2003.

Conason, Joe, *The Longest Con: How Grifters, Swindlers, and Frauds Hijacked American Conservatism.* New York, New York: St. Martin's Press, 2024.

Conason, Joe, and Gene Lyons, *The Hunting of the Presidency: The Ten-Year Campaign to Destroy Bill and Hillary Clinton.* New York, New York: St. Martin's Press, 2000.

Conason, Joe, Gene Lyons, and Nickolas Perry, *The Hunting of the President*, directed by Nickolas Perry and Harry Thomason, 2004; Los Angeles, California: Regent Releasing, Amazon Prime Video.

Coppins, McKay, "Here's The 'Willie Horton' Ad Romney Almost Ran Against Mike Huckabee," BuzzFeed News, January 22, 2015. https://www.buzzfeednews.com/article/mckaycoppins/heres-the-willie-horton-ad-romney-almost-ran-against-mike-hu#.jikjEkBe

Corn, David, "Here Come the Crazy Clinton Conspiracies of the 1990s," *Mother Jones*, February 20, 2014. https://www.motherjones.com/politics/2014/02/clinton-conspiracy-theories-kathleen-willey-chronicles/

Crowley, Michael, "Trump's long dalliance with violent rhetoric," Politico.com, August 10, 2016. https://www.politico.com/story/2016/08/trump-violent-rhetoric-history-226873

D'Antonio, Michael, *The Hunting of Hillary: The Forty-Year Campaign to Destroy Hillary Clinton,* New York, New York: St. Martin's Press, 2020.

Davis, John, *From Blue to Red: The Rise of the GOP in Arkansas.* Fayetteville, Arkansas: The University of Arkansas Press, 2024.

Dickey, Colin, "From Sound of Freedom to Ron DeSantis: How QAnon's crazy conspiracy theories went mainstream," *The Guardian*, August 16, 2023. https://

www.theguardian.com/us-news/2023/aug/16/qanon-conspiracy-theory-sound-of-freedom-trump-desantis

Duin, Julia. "The Christian Prophets Who Say Trump Is Coming Again," Politico.com, February 18, 2021. https://www.politico.com/news/magazine/2021/02/18/how-christian-prophets-give-credence-to-trumps-election-fantasies-469598

Dumas, Ernest, "Bill Clinton," The Encyclopedia of Arkansas. https://encyclopediaofarkansas.net/entries/bill-clinton-95/

Dumas, Ernest, "Wayne Eugene Dumond," The Encyclopedia of Arkansas. https://encyclopediaofarkansas.net/entries/wayne-eugene-dumond-8005/

Dumas, Ernest, "Whitewater Scandal," The Encyclopedia of Arkansas, July 29, 2024. https://encyclopediaofarkansas.net/entries/whitewater-scandal-4061/

Dunleavy, Steve, "Clinton's Biggest Crime: Left Innocent Man in Jail for 14 Years," New York Post, September 21, 1999. https://nypost.com/1999/09/21/clintons-biggest-crime-left-innocent-man-in-jail-for-14-years/

Duleavy, Steve. "I Sure Hope Bill's No Rapist." New York Post, February 22, 1999. https://infoweb-newsbank-com.eu1.proxy.openathens.net/apps/news/document-view?p=AMNEWS&docref=news/15AF8AADAACC0248.

Falk, William, "Why Fox News was created," The Week, November 22, 2019. https://theweek.com/articles/880107/why-fox-news-created

"Farm to Table," Diners, Drive-Ins, and Dives, Season 9 Episode 9, aired June 27, 2010. Food Network.

Farmer, Joe, "Parole board hears Dumond's side," Arkansas Democrat, September 13, 1990.

Feinberg, Ayal, Regina Branton, and Valerie Martinez-Ebers, "Counties that hosted a 2016 Trump rally saw a 226 percent increase in hate crimes," *The Washington Post*, March 22, 2019. https://www.washingtonpost.com/politics/2019/03/22/trumps-rhetoric-does-inspire-more-hate-crimes/

Ferguson, Greg, and David Bowermaster, "Whatever it is, Bill Clinton Likely Did It," *U.S. News & World Report,* August 8, 1994. https://www.govinfo.gov/content/pkg/CREC-1994-08-12/html/CREC-1994-08-12-pt1-PgE40.htm

Fisher, Mark, John Woodrow Cox, and Peter Herman, "Pizzagate: From rumor, to hashtag, to gunfire in D.C.," *The Washington Post*, December 6, 2016. https://www.washingtonpost.com/local/pizzagate-from-rumor-to-hashtag-to-gunfire-in-dc/2016/12/06/4c7def50-bbd4-11e6-94ac-3d324840106c_story.html

Green, Joshua, *Devil's Bargain: Steve Bannon, Donald Trump, and the Storming of the Presidency,* New York, New York: Penguin Press, 2017.

Goldman, Adam, "Ping Pong Gunman Answers Our Reporter's Questions," *New York Times*, December 7, 2016. https://www.nytimes.com/2016/12/07/us/edgar-welch-comet-pizza-fake-news.html

Hardy, Benjamin, "Activist 'Say' McIntosh, Little Rock's 'sweet potato pie king,' is dead at 79," *Arkansas Times*, June 26, 2023. https://arktimes.com/arkansas-blog/2023/06/26/activist-say-mcintosh-little-rocks-sweet-potato-pie-king-is-dead-at-79

Harkavy, Ward, "The Castration of Wayne Dumond," *The Village Voice*, March 6, 2001. file:///Users/marcogutierrez/Desktop/Wayne%20Dumond/Clinton%20CTIC/The%20Castration%20of%20

Wayne%20DuMond%20-%20The%20Village%20
Voice.html

"Hate Group Expert Daniel Levitas Discusses Posse Comitatus, Christian Identity Movement and More," *Intelligence Report,* June 15, 1998. https://www. splcenter.org/fighting-hate/intelligence-report/1998/ hate-group-expert-daniel-levitas-discusses-posse-comitatus-christian-identity-movement-and

Helling, David, "Mothers hold Huckabee partially responsible for daughters' murders," McClatchy DC, December 4, 2007. https://www.mcclatchydc.com/ news/politics-government/article24472912.html

Hendry, Erica R., "Trump asked Russia to find Clinton's emails. On or around the same day, Russia targeted her accounts," *PBS News,* July 13, 2018. https:// www.pbs.org/newshour/politics/trump-asked-russia-to-find-clintons-emails-on-or-around-the-same-day-russians-targeted-her-accounts

Hill, Jack, interviewer, *In Focus.* "Hillary Rodham interview," aired January 1979. https://www.youtube. com/watch?v=bg_sEZg7-rk&t=3s

Hill, Jack, "'Knew' sheriff wasn't telling truth, Dumond's wife says," *Arkansas Democrat,* April 17, 1986.

Hill, Jack E., "Wins on Stump, Records Citing Days as Gambler Precede New Conlee Bid," *Arkansas Democrat*, April 27, 1986.

Hoback, Cullen, director, *Into the Storm*, Season 1, Episode 1: "Calm Before the Storm," aired March 21, 2021, on HBO Max.

Hoback, Cullen, director, *Into the Storm*, Season 1, Episode 3: "Disinformation Is Real," aired March 21, 2021, on HBO Max.

Hoback, Cullen, director, *Into the Storm*, Season 1, Episode 4: "Panic in D.C.," aired March 21, 2021, on HBO Max.

Hoback, Cullen, director, Into the Storm, Season 1, Episode 5: "Game Over," aired March 21, 2021, on HBO Max.

Hoback, Cullen, director, *Into the Storm*, Season 1, Episode 6: "The Storm," aired March 21, 2021, on HBO Max.

Huckabee, Mike, address to the 5th Annual Meeting of the Conservative Political Action Committee, February 10, 2008. https://www.americanrhetoric.com/speeches/mikehuckabee2008cpac.htm

Huckabee, Mike, with John Perry, *Character IS the Issue: How People with Integrity Can Revolutionize America,* Nashville, Tennessee: Broadman & Holman Publishers, 1997.

Huckabee, Mike, *Do the Right Thing: Inside the Movement That's Bringing Common Sense Back to America,* New York, New York: Penguin Group, 2008.

"Jay Daniel Cole (1929-2011)," FindaGrave.com.

Jester, Scott, "A Boyhood Fascination Results in Lifelong Broadcasting Career," HopePrescott.com, May 6, 2022. https://hopeprescott.com/2022/05/06/a-boyhood-facination-results-in-lifelong-broadcasting-career-how-jerry-westmoreland-has-used-voice-to-be-servant-of-citizens-and-his-community/

Jones, Robert P., "What White Christians Have Wrought," *Time*, November 11, 2024. https://time.com/7174260/white-christianity-trump-election-essay/?utm_medium=email&utm_source=sfmc&utm_campaign=newsletter+brief+default+ac&utm_content=+++20241116+++body&et_rid=207459329&lctg=207459329

Kaczynski, Andrew, "Romney Vetoed Ad Linking Huckabee To Woman's Death," BuzzFeed News, August 10, 2012. https://www.buzzfeednews.com/article/andrewkaczynski/romney-vetoed-ad-linking-huckabee-to-womans-death#.cowyaPMxx

Kaylor, Brian, "A 'Transformative Moment' in SBC Political Activity," Good Faith Media, August 20, 2010. https://goodfaithmedia.org/a-transformative-moment-in-sbc-political-activity-cms-16555/

Keaton, Bryce, "Fake News Killed Carol Sue Shields," YouTube video, 29:42. January 22, 2018. https://youtu.be/APNMitAM71s.

Keaton, Bryce, in discussion with the author, January 2021.

Kellams, Kyle, "A Bizarre Criminal Case, Decades Later," KUAF, June 12, 2023. Accessed December 29, 2023, at https://www.kuaf.com/show/ozarks-at-large/2023-06-12/a-bizarre-criminal-case-decades-later

Kellams, Kyle, "Part 2 of a Bizarre Criminal Case, Decades Later," KUAF, June 19, 2023. Accessed December 29, 2023, at https://www.kuaf.com/show/ozarks-at-large/2023-06-19/part-2-of-bizarre-a-criminal-case-decades-later

Kellams, Kyle, "The odd story of Coolidge Conley," KUAF, June 26, 2023. Accessed December 29, 2023, at https://www.kuaf.com/show/ozarks-at-large/2023-06-26/the-odd-story-of-sheriff-coolidge-conley.

Koon, David, "The Says of our lives," *Arkansas Times*, October 5, 2011. https://arktimes.com/news/cover-stories/2011/10/05/the-says-of-our-livesLau, Tim, "Citizens United Explained," Brennan Center for Justice, December 12, 2019.

Liptak, Adam, "Justices, 5-4, Reject Corporate Spending Limit," *The New York Times*, January 21, 2010. https://

www.nytimes.com/2010/01/22/us/politics/22scotus.
html

Lyon, Georgia, "How Does the Citizens United Decision Still Affect Us in 2024?" CampaignLegal.org, January 24, 2024. https://campaignlegal.org/update/how-does-citizens-united-decision-still-affect-us-2024

Lyons, Gene, "Fool for Scandal: How the 'Times' Got Whitewater Wrong," *Harper's Magazine*, October 1994. Archived at: https://www.pbs.org/wgbh/pages/frontline/shows/arkansas/whitewater/lyonsarticle.html

Lyons, Gene, "The roots of the Clinton smear," Salon.com, February 5, 1998. https://www.salon.com/1998/02/05/cov_05news/

"Manual," Militia of Washington County Arkansas. https://www.angelfire.com/ar2/militia/

Maraniss, David, "Before Race Began, Clinton Resolved Pledge Not to Run," *The Washington Post,* July 14, 1992. Accessed at https://www.washingtonpost.com/archive/politics/1992/07/15/before-race-began-clinton-resolved-pledge-not-to-run/696cb650-3dab-4fcc-97dd-8bdcbb4b50f5/

Marcotte, Amanda, "The Clinton BS Files: "Lock her up" isn't really about emails — the right's been accusing the Clintons of murder for decades," Salon.com, August 29, 2016. https://www.salon.com/2016/08/29/the-clinton-bs-files-lock-her-up-isnt-really-about-emails-the-rights-been-accusing-the-clintons-of-murder-for-decades/

Marcotte, Amanda, "The Clinton BS files: The right wing's long history of obsession with the Clintons' sex lives," Salon.com, August 22, 2016. https://www.salon.

com/2016/08/22/the-clinton-bs-files-the-right-wings-long-history-of-obsession-with-the-clintons-sex-lives/

Matthews, Dylan, "The conspiracy theories about the Clintons and Jeffrey Epstein's death, explained," *Vox*, November 14, 2019. https://www.vox.com/2019/8/10/20800195/clintonbodycount-conspiracy-theory-jeffrey-epstein

Media Matters, "Dick Morris misrepresented facts of DuMond case in purporting to explain Huckabee's focus," December 12, 2007. Accessed January 9, 2024, at https://www.mediamatters.org/sean-hannity/dick-morris-misrepresented-facts-dumond-case-purporting-explain-huckabees-focus

Meisel, Jan, "Fears Dumond, victim testifies," *Arkansas Democrat*, September 5, 1990.

Miller, Cassie, "The Violent History of the Anti-Abortion Movement," *The Intelligence Report*, June 13, 2024. https://www.splcenter.org/anti-abortion-movement/violent-history

Miller, Michael, "The Pizzagate gunman is out of prison. Conspiracy theories are out of control." *Seattle Times*, February 16, 2021. https://www.seattletimes.com/nation-world/the-pizzagate-gunman-is-out-of-prison-conspiracy-theories-are-out-of-control/

Mute. Kathy Sue Holtorf, director. Edgar Maddison Welch, writer. 2011. YouTube, 8:40. Accessed June 1, 2024 at https://youtu.be/RQrvNiFWPDo?si=4Edeh3miD7AMB69x

Nasaw, David, "The Arkansas businessman who bought Governor Huckabee flowers and suits," *The Guardian*, December 13, 2007. https://www.theguardian.com/world/2007/dec/13/usa.danielnasaw

"No leads in castration case," UPI, March 9, 1985. https://www.upi.com/Archives/1985/03/09/ No-leads-in-castration-case/1658479192400/

Oreskes, Michael, "Political Memo; For G.O.P. Arsenal, 133 Words to Fire," *The New York Times*, September 9, 1990. Archived at: https://web.archive.org/web/20120129074440/http://www.nytimes.com/1990/09/09/us/political-memo-for-gop-arsenal-133-words-to-fire.html

"Overview: The Rise of Talk Radio," PBS.org, July 12, 2005. http://archive.pov.org/thefirenexttime/overview-the-rise-of-talk-radio/

Parker, Suzi, "Huckabee's Feud With The Clintons," *The Daily Beast*, April 14, 2017. https://www.thedailybeast.com/huckabees-feud-with-the-clintons

"Parole of Rapist Stirs Resentment, Fear in Hometown." News at 6, September 27, 1999. https://www.newson6.com/story/5e36864f2f69d76f6209bf47/parole-of-rapist-stirs-resentment-fear-in-hometown

PBS NewsHour, "Watch the second presidential debate between Hillary Clinton and Donald Trump," YouTube video, October 9, 2016. 1:56:52. https://www.youtube.com/live/IcNyCmBTJCY?si=Usoj17pSyw377SfA

Hillary: The Movie, Alan Peterson, director, Citizens United, 2008. 1:30:16. https://youtu.be/tn8kyRQKmEk?si=bXpVTrBJnt99-0C5

"The Politics of Slash and Burn," *The New York Times Opinion*, September 20, 1990. Archived at: https://web.archive.org/web/20111205134229/http://www.nytimes.com/1990/09/20/opinion/the-politics-of-slash-and-burn.html?src=pm

"The Press: The Machine Wins," *Time Magazine*, February 11, 1966. https://content.time.com/time/subscriber/article/0,33009,842472,00.html

"The Press: Variety of Violence," *Time Magazine*, February 11, 1966. https://content.time.com/time/subscriber/article/0,33009,873420,00.html

Ramsey, David, "Former Clinton foe comes back to Arkansas to defend the Clintons," *Arkansas Times*, March 25, 2014. https://arktimes.com/arkansas-blog/2014/03/25/former-clinton-foe-david-brock-comes-back-to-arkansas-to-defend-the-clintons

Reel, Guy, personal interview with the author, February 14, 2024.

Reel, Guy, *Unequal Justice: Wayne Dumond, Bill Clinton, and the Politics of Rape in Arkansas,* Buffalo, New York: Prometheus Books, 1993.

Rice, Glenn E., "Killer's death short-circuits '01 case," *Kansas City Star*, September 2, 2005. https://web.archive.org/web/20071207145110/http://blogs.kansascity.com/crime_scene/2005/09/killers_death_s.html

Robb, Amanda, "Anatomy of a Fake News Scandal," *Rolling Stone*, November 16, 2017. https://www.rollingstone.com/feature/anatomy-of-a-fake-news-scandal-125877/

Rosencrance, Linda. "Former Ark. governor hit with ethics complaint over destroyed hard drives." *Computerworld*, February 2, 2007.

Rosin, Hanna, "What's Huck Hiding? Searching for the lost Huckabee tapes," Slate.com, February 21, 2008. https://slate.com/news-and-politics/2008/02/my-search-for-the-lost-huckabee-tapes.html

Sabin, Warwick, "The Hunting of the President," *Arkansas Times*, June 10, 2004. https://arktimes.com/news/cover-stories/2004/06/10/the-hunting-of-the-president

"The saga of 'Pizzagate': The fake story that shows how conspiracy theories spread," BBC Trending, December 2, 2016. https://www.bbc.com/news/blogs-trending-38156985?ocid=socialflow_facebook&ns_mchannel=social&ns_campaign=bbcnewsmagazine&ns_source=facebook&fbclid=IwZXh0bgNhZW0CMTEAAR2n4-C1nTyp4a7c9IKM_9a6LHyvmhKnMF9FcG7GtuBeE7zelgIrD4ip9gA_aem_ASvY4Xv2ip2ubj606w4koEoxm7iJ9u956VAwEooTIN9Rz-FFlgLbvv_sNZ4rjMQOassz1mt2KApqGiCjqIfNWw70

Sarlo, Aaron, "Tucker flips, flops," *Arkansas Times*, July 16, 1996. https://arktimes.com/columns/max-brantley/1996/07/19/tucker-flips-flops?oid=3894507

Save Our Nation, "Jay D. Cole." Accessed at http://www.saveournation.net/founder.htm.

Serrano, Richard A., "Parole officials: Huckabee pushed rapist's release," *Los Angeles Times*, December 8, 2007.

Shalev, Chemi, "The Conspiracy Theory About the FBI Putsch Against Clinton and Democracy," *Haaretz*, November 4, 2016. https://www.haaretz.com/world-news/2016-11-04/ty-article/the-conspiracy-theory-about-the-fbi-putsch-against-clinton-and-democracy/0000017f-e60b-d62c-a1ff-fe7b40220000

Special Collections, Jack E. Hill Papers, Series 3, Boxes 41-43.

State v. Dumond, WD 63710, (Mo. Ct. App. Sep. 13, 2005).

Stearns, Matt, "Rumors shroud suspect's record," *The Kansas City Star*, July 1, 2001.

Stein, Jonathan and David Corn, "Huckabee Hides His Full Gospel?" *Mother Jones*, December 10, 2007. https://www.motherjones.com/politics/2007/12/huckabee-hides-his-full-gospel/

Sullivan, Bartholomew, "Dumond Linked to Missouri Slaying; Kansas City Cops Search Home, Worksite," *The Commercial Appeal*, June 26, 2001. https://www.proquest.com/central/newspapers/dumond-linked-missouri-slayingkansas-city-cops/docview/393923751/sem-2?accountid=8361

Taylor, Jessica, "More Surprises: FBI Releases Files On Bill Clinton's Pardon Of Marc Rich," NPR.org, November 1, 2016. https://www.npr.org/2016/11/01/500297580/more-surprises-fbi-releases-files-on-bill-clintons-pardon-of-marc-rich

Teske, Steven, "Cuban Refugee Crisis," The Encyclopedia of Arkansas.

Toobin, Jeffrey, "Ashcroft's Ascent," *The New Yorker*, April 7, 2002. Accessed at: https://www.newyorker.com/magazine/2002/04/15/ashcrofts-ascent

Vazquez, Maegan, "Trump again refuses to denounce QAnon," CNN.com, October 15, 2020. https://www.cnn.com/2020/10/15/politics/donald-trump-qanon-town-hall/index.html

Victims Voice, "If not for Mike Huckabee... Carol Sue Shields would be with us," YouTube, January 1, 2008. 0:57. https://youtu.be/Y18NQcByIyI?si=rHCUlLOc2nnqeMF8

Vogel, Kenneth P., "Huckabee rivals unearth ethics complaints," *Politico*, November 21, 2007. Updated November 23, 2007. https://www.politico.com/story/2007/11/huckabee-rivals-unearth-ethics-complaints-007000

Waas, Murray S., "Arkansas trooper considered demanding money from President Clinton," Salon.com, April 9, 1998. https://www.salon.com/1998/04/09/news_18/

Waas, Murray S., "Documents Expose Huckabee's Role in Serial Rapist's Release," Huffington Post, March 28, 2008. https://www.huffpost.com/entry/documents-expose-huckabee_n_75362

Waas, Murray S., "Web special: Dumond case revisited," *Arkansas Times*, 2002, updated September 1, 2005. https://web.archive.org/web/20071212042550/http://www.arktimes.com/Articles/ArticleViewer.aspx?ArticleID=154e1aad-fd18-4efd-8d80-b5dab8559419

Watson, Russell, "Vince Foster's Suicide: The Rumor Mill Churns," *Newsweek*, March 20, 1994. Updated March 13, 2010. https://www.newsweek.com/vince-fosters-suicide-rumor-mill-churns-185900

Weiss, Phillip, "Clinton Crazy," *The New York Times Magazine*, February 23, 1997, Sec. 6, p. 35. https://www.nytimes.com/1997/02/23/magazine/clinton-crazy.html

Wirges, Gene, *Conflict of Interests: The Gene Wirges Story,* North Little Rock, Arkansas: Riverboat Publishers, 1992.

Woodward, Colin, "Cummins Unit," Encyclopedia of Arkansas, June 16, 2023. Accessed at https://encyclopediaofarkansas.net/entries/cummins-unit-7607/

WUSA9, "Raw: 'Pizzagate' suspect records message to his family on way to DC," posted June 22, 2017. YouTube, 1:44. https://youtu.be/vhRo_jFKf9M?si=4elhdO0CyH6k6Ta7